Living in and Visitin[g]

100 Tips, Tricks, Traps

Greg Seymour

First Print Edition

Seymour Sunsets Publishing
CostaRicaCurious@icloud.com

www.CostaRicaCurious.com

For Jen

My partner in this great adventure, life.

TABLE OF CONTENTS

PREFACE

"Upwards of 40% of expats, with the intention of making a permanent move to Costa Rica, will return to the country of their origin within the first year."

This statement is often made on expat websites, videos and other media. It is never backed up with verified numbers (how could it be?), but nevertheless it is used. The reality is no one really knows, but my guess is that it is a relatively close estimation.

That means for every ten people who move here, four will not celebrate their first anniversary as expats in Costa Rica. Four will have spent up to $20,000 (or more) in travel, shipping and starting the process of becoming residents in Costa Rica.

The reasons that people don't make it here the first year are many but for the majority who leave within the first year, it boils down to lack of knowledge, insufficient preparation, and an inability to adjust to a new culture.

I imagine it is because there is so much information out there about Costa Rica that some do not feel they need to research it. They get here and then find out that Costa Rica is not just a version of the U.S. several years behind – a North America Lite - it's actually a foreign country.

With my wife Jen and I both writing blogs (mine is: www.CostaRicaCurious.com and hers is: www.CostaRicaChica.com) we get plenty of questions from readers. Some of them are really basic, like "Where should I live?" and "What is the weather like?" which is fine except when these questions are preceded by the declaration, "I am moving to Costa Rica in three months."

I am not kidding.

My wife and I have been here for over a year and a half and have passed that scary one-year mark – we are in THE 60%! I feel so fortunate. Really, I do not. All in all we spent two years from the time we thought retiring to a foreign country could be an option for us, to the time that we moved. We used this time to visit Costa Rica, learn about the culture and those things that might be a challenge for us, to sell all but nine suitcases worth of stuff, and to wrap up our careers in Dallas.

For the first time tourist, Costa Rica can be a wonderland of nature and culture. Not really addressing the all-inclusive crowd (which in Costa Rica could be compared to keeping your Ferrari in the garage and only driving it once in a while, and then only on neighborhood streets) this book will help you acclimate to some of the quirks of non-tourist areas, so you can take the country out for a spin and maximize your adventure.

The reason I wrote this book is not to convince you to move to or visit Costa Rica, or to convince you otherwise. I have no skin in this game and I honestly don't care what you do. I wrote this book because it was the type of book I was looking for, and couldn't find, when Jen and I were researching if Costa Rica was right for us.

…and I wrote it to fund my ever growing *chicharrón* habit.

Before moving, we had read obsessively about the subject of Costa Rica and moving here. Some of the books gave us information, some gave us a laugh or a story, and some made us groan. What we did not find was a book that was heavy on observations and personal experiences. Sure there were the stale travel guides that could make a spaceship ride sound boring, then the travelogues that were more personal but still lacked real-world, daily-life information, and other books on Costa Rica fell short as well. So, this missing book is the one I wrote.

The book is filled with the observations and experiences of someone living in and with Costa Rica daily as an expat, not a tourist. I don't take myself, or my writing, too seriously and you will notice, throughout the book, I take a humorous approach to both life here and life in general.

I begin the book with a chapter telling the short version of our story - why we chose to move to another country for early retirement.

The remaining chapters cover topics like what to expect at: The Bank, The Grocery Store, The Restaurant, The Restroom, when Driving or Taking the Bus, and more. At the end of the book I even give you some unfiltered opinions – lucky you!

Each chapter provides tips, tricks, traps or facts on its subject; when possible I provide a story of how we learned a particular piece of information.

This book is not intended to be exhaustive; instead it is a snap shot, a slice of expat (a person living in a foreign country) life in Costa Rica, to show some of the quirks of living in Central America, or visiting in the less touristy areas so that you will be better prepared for the cultural and day-to-day differences from North America.

And yes, I realize everyone who reads this book is not from North America. But the majority will be, and I write from a USA'ian perspective, so there.

This book targets both the visitor to Costa Rica and the hopeful expat. For the visitor, the tips, tricks, traps, and facts will help lessen the learning curve so that he can start enjoying Costa Rica faster and get more out of his short time here. For those looking for a retirement destination, I hope these hundred items will inspire and inform you, giving you a better chance at being a member of the 60%.

Acknowledgments

I have never written for public consumption - outside of writing my blog www.CostaRicaCurious.com (available worldwide, wherever an Internet connect can be found) that is. Remembering all those pesky little things like correct word usage, grammar, where the commas and apostrophes go, and other annoying punctuational rules was just about impossible for me.

Without the help of the friends listed below, this book would be a mess.

The first line of defense, the team that saw the worst of what I call writing, was my wife Jen "lose the Caps babe" Seymour and friend Lynette Hunt. These ladies received a very rough draft and once they returned it with corrections, I said, "Damn, I can write."

Paul and Gloria Yeatman provided their expertise and knowledge of living in Costa Rica for six years to ensure I got all the facts right – I didn't. The Yeatmans write a website: www.retireforlessincostarica.com and on it they demonstrate how they live an incredible life in Costa Rica on less than they did in the States. They also offer healthcare and retirement/relocation tours of the Central Valley. If you stop by their site tell them I said hi.

Last, and certainly not least, Ken Cline agreed to edit the book when it was only 50 tips, tricks, traps, and facts. When I finally gave him the completed book it was about 12,000 words more than the draft I had originally sent him to preview. And still he took on the project…

while he was on vacation. Thanks too to Bina, Ken's wife, who assisted with the editing process.

When (not if) you find an error in the book, it's mine. I have a tendency of not leaving well enough alone.... And then not having someone look it over again. Ha.

Above all, I want to thank the individuals above for their encouragement and enthusiasm for my first book.

You all are rock stars.

CHAPTER 1 – How we got here

It was 2011 when the wear and stress at my job started to show, both in my physical and mental health.

I was the Vice President of a division of a company that was in decline; the division was in decline, not the company. The company was stronger than ever.

In essence I was the captain of a sinking ship – managing a division whose purpose was no longer to make money but to be a loss leader for more profitable business units within the company. While my management responsibilities were increasing, my pay was decreasing. I was expected to get the same amount of work done, but with fewer employees.

My wife and I had both built successful careers and had chosen early in our marriage not to have children (gasp), so we had built our lives around a large disposable income. I used this disposable income to fund my stress-coping mechanisms – food and drink.

My weight had ballooned, as had the milligram dosage of my blood pressure medication. I was stressed and depressed and at some moment of clarity I knew that if I did not make a change soon I was going to start having some serious medical issues.

My solution – let's move to a country we have never been to before.

I am a dreamer and this solution, as played out in my head, was both rational and executable. The only problem was, I was married. Married to a woman much more pragmatic than I. So, while I had solved this problem by determining the solution before doing the research, I really could not go forward without involving Jen.

The smart thing to do, of course, was to exhaust all our options stateside before considering a move abroad. First we discussed me finding another job. Throughout the 22 years I spent working in my industry, I had only worked for three different companies. Even though the market I was in was specialized, I had been able to hone skills that could transfer to many other companies and industries: Recruiting, Training, Production Management, Sales Management and Operations Management. Basically any job that required finding, training, and getting work done through others in an efficient manner was a candidate for my skill set. I also knew that there was a place for me at my current company, in a different capacity, if I desired.

I did not desire.

The truth is I really no longer liked what I was doing and was really tired of being responsible for someone else's, or 40 others', actions and inactions. Added to that, my company's main client category was attorneys, litigation attorneys, to be precise. I had really grown to dislike the late nights and weekend work associated with supporting firms going to trial, not to mention enduring the "special" personality traits of trial teams. So, finding another similar job in the same industry or retooling my skills with my employer was a non-starter.

Next, we considered buying a company or starting a business from scratch, and quickly decided against that as well. There was just too much risk, and not to sound lazy, too much work. I was leaving a career where my base day was 10 hours long and it only went up from there. I was tired, and starting a business would have just continued that trend.

We considered moving to a smaller town and downsizing. We were concerned about downsizing where we lived, in Dallas, because we had developed a lifestyle and a group of friends that, right or wrong, we didn't feel would transition with such a change.

We (read: I) considered buying an RV and taking off on a North American tour. In a similar vein, we (I) considered buying a sailboat and sailing around the world, at least to the Caribbean. This last one is most amusing because I had never sailed before. Hell, I had never even been on a sailboat. Oh, and I stand at a height of 6'4". Add to the equation a wife, who does not like being on the open sea or gallivanting around in an RV, and you can see why we (she) quickly shelved those ideas.

It was at this time, after we had scratched off most of our "move on" options, that I purchased a book on living cheaply in a foreign country. I drooled over descriptions of cheap beer and practically free fruits and vegetables, never mind that I don't like vegetables.

I read the book as if it were actually a possibility to move away from Dallas, from the United States, from the only culture I had ever known. I read the book as if not having to work was an option.

I dreamt.

Jen of course thought I was crazy. She was probably right, but I talked about it so much that she started showing an interest in the subject of moving to foreign countries, and that offered me a flicker of hope.

As I read the descriptions of countries and their various merits and disadvantages, I mentally crossed off areas of the world in which it would be impractical (as if they were not all impractical) to live. Asia – too far from the States and I really had no desire to learn about Asian culture. Europe – wow. Europe would be awesome, but for the most part Europe seemed too far away and too expensive to consider.

I basically ended up with Latin America and the Caribbean, and upon further research and reflection I whittled the world down to include only the following countries: Belize, Costa Rica, Panama and Ecuador.

I determined that Ecuador was too far away from Dallas. My dad was in poor health at the time and we wanted to be living somewhere that was within a few hours flight to Dallas.

Belize seemed too much like North America to me, using the U.S. dollar as its currency and English as its official language. The beach seemed to be where most expats lived in Belize; I wanted to live in a country that had multiple climate options. It looked like Panama and Costa Rica were the only two countries left on my list that provided all the "must haves" that I was looking for.

I figured now would be a good time to tell Jen that we were moving to Central America.

I have a tendency to build grandiose plans in my head and share these plans with my wife as if they were reality. Jen knows this about me and she takes these thoughts with the requisite spoonful of salt. After a couple of weeks had gone by and I was still blabbing on and on about retiring to a foreign country, Jen's passing interest in the subject turned to serious questions about moving away.

It had been several years since we had taken more than a weeklong vacation so we figured we were due one. We started planning a 2-country trip, one week in Panama, and one week in Costa Rica. We would spend time in 2 or 3 locations in each country and really try to work out whether it would be a fit for us and vice versa. We would do this by staying in towns we would want to live in (i.e., not at resorts) and spend our time meeting locals and expats.

I am not sure what happened to Panama, but as we were researching places to visit and things to do, Panama fell off our radar and our trip became entirely about Costa Rica. This is surprising because we were considering retiring early and cost of living was a huge component of that plan. It was clear that Panama was less expensive on just about every front.

In addition to having cheaper staple items (food, the all important beer, rent and utilities), the Panamanian government seemed to woo the expat with incentives for those applying for residency. Residents were treated to benefits such as being able to import a vehicle into the country without paying duty and importing a large amount of household goods without incurring duty costs as well.

Costa Rica really offered no benefit for an expat becoming a resident other than not having to leave the country every 90 days to renew the tourist visa. In fact that same car that incurred no duty when shipped to Panama would cost 50 – 75% of the value of the vehicle (depending on age) in duties alone, if shipped to Costa Rica.

Whatever the reason, we were turned off by Panama and our trip to investigate a place to retire turned into a one-country trip. Talk about putting all your eggs in one basket.

In January of 2012, Jen and I, and for good measure (and good judgment), Jen's mom, flew into Juan Santamaría Airport (SJO) near the Costa Rican capital city San José. Our trip was ten days long and during the trip we would experience three different living environments.

We chose to visit Grecia, a small farming town, to give us a vibe of the Central Valley. We visited the beaches of Guanacaste in the northwest corner of the country (Playa Hermosa, Conchal, Flamingo and Playas del Coco) to give us the flavor of beach life. Finally, we rounded out the trip by visiting the Lake Arenal/Nuevo Arenal/La Fortuna area to sample the rainforest.

As we had planned, we spend the bulk of the trip learning about Costa Rica, its people, culture, and places we might want to live. We stayed away from tourist activities and for two of our days hired an expat couple to show us around. This was money well spent, as we were able to meet with doctors, a veterinarian, price shop in different venues, and basically get all of our questions answered from someone who had lived in Costa Rica for several years.

A couple of months after this trip, we had decided that, yes, we would retire early and move to Costa Rica. One and a half years after that decision we moved to Costa Rica. We decided on the consistently great weather and views afforded in the Central Valley as our new home; Grecia to be specific.

This book is not really about our story, but I wanted to give you a quick low down of how we ended up living in Costa Rica. I have written this book to share some of the things we learned, both on that initial trip and in our first year and a half of living in this foreign country.

I am not a very well traveled person. A couple of trips to the two countries that sandwich the United States, and a cruise to the Bahamas was the extent of my world travels prior to visiting Costa Rica for the first time. I mention this because some of my observations may seem pedestrian to the well-traveled soul.

Forgive me.

My experiences here are mostly based in the Central Valley area of Costa Rica so some of my observations may differ from those of someone who visits a different part of the country (or the same part of the country on a different day).

My dad used to always say, "learn the system", and where there is one, I will certainly tell you about it; but occasionally it seems there is not a system in place here or that it changes with wind or whim.

So, as they say, your mileage may vary.

CHAPTER 2 – The rich coast

It is unknown who named this Central American country *la costa rica* – "the rich coast." Most likely it was either Christopher Columbus, who reached Costa Rica, on the Caribbean side, in 1502 or the conquistador Gil González Dávila, who traveled to Costa Rica in 1522.

While the country does have a tremendous amount of natural resources, precious metals are not a large part of them, and whoever named the country did so out of mistaking Costa Rica for a metals-rich country or to save face from a busted expedition.

Gold or no gold, this small country packs a wallop when it comes to diversity in nature, climate, and geography.

Let's start the Tips, Tricks, Traps, and Facts off with some facts and observations about Costa Rica and her people that make it such an interesting country to live in or visit.

1. Size

Costa Rica is a small country in Central America that has a size of about 51,000 sq. km (you know you are going to have to (re)learn the metric system, right?). The U.S. state most often used as an equivalent to Costa Rica's size is West Virginia, which is about 1,500 sq. km. larger than the Rich Coast.

The country is roughly 450 km. in length (North – South) and 275 km. in width (West – East). Costa Rica is bordered to the North by Nicaragua, on the Southeast by Panama, on the West by the Pacific Ocean, and on the East by the Caribbean Sea.

Costa Rica's population in 2013 was almost 4.9 million, with the country's two neighbors, Nicaragua and Panama weighing in at 6 and 3.8 million respectively.

It is estimated that a full three-quarters of the population lives in the Central Valley (this includes one-quarter, over a million people, living in San José, the capital city, and its environs).

Estimates vary but Costa Rica has about 1,200 km. of shoreline (1,000 on the Pacific side and 200 on the Caribbean side) with nearly 300 beaches where you can work on your tan or practice falling off a surfboard.

Please note, the shoreline is only on two sides making Costa Rica an isthmus, not an…

2. The number one misconception about Costa Rica

Despite unbelievably widespread misperceptions, Costa Rica is not an island. Maybe it's believed to be so because of the country's tropical climate. Maybe it is because so much emphasis is placed on Costa Rica's beaches. Maybe it's because of the culture of pura vida – that laid back, life is good, things will happen when they happen attitude, known elsewhere as "island time."

Whatever the reason, the country is commonly thought to be an island.

Not only do people think Costa Rica is an island, they think it is a territory of the United States, not a country. In the end, people confuse Costa Rica with Puerto Rico - probably because the name shares the partial word "Ric."

3. This land is your land

Costa Rica may be a small country but it is world class in its conservation efforts. A full 25% of the country's landmass is protected land.

Part of this protected land is used in the national parks system, for wildlife refuges, forest and biological reserves.

Tourism as a whole is Costa Rica's number one source of income. Eco-tourism, as a subset, continues to grow at a rapid pace.

4. Ring of fire

Costa Rica is a land born of volcanoes and it's no wonder; Costa Rica sits in the Pacific Ring of Fire, a 25,000-mile, horseshoe-shaped area known for its volcanic and seismic activity. Johnny Cash would be proud.

Costa Rica can be divided into four mountain ranges: Central Volcanic Range, Talamanca Range, Tilarán and Guanacaste. Within the confines of this small country reside at least 200 volcanic formations, half of which show some volcanic activity.

Most of Costa Rica's volcanoes are located in the Central Volcanic Range and the Guanacaste Range. Below is a list of the most popular volcanoes in these two ranges.

Central Volcano Range:
Poás Volcano
Irazú Volcano
Barva Volcano
Turrialba Volcano

Guanacaste Range:
Arenal Volcano
Orosí Volcano
Rincón de la Vieja Volcano
Tenorio Volcano

Many of these volcanoes are national parks and you can visit and see the volcanoes up close. The most popular from a tourism perspective are Arenal and Poás.

5. Shake, rattle and roll

Keeping with the theme of natural phenomenon let's talk about earthquakes. Earthquakes are a frequent visitor to Costa Rica and they can occur anywhere within the country.

According to www.volcanodiscovery.com, Costa Rica saw (felt) 69 earthquakes in 2014 that were a magnitude of or greater than 4.2.

Earthquakes in Costa Rica can be caused either by tectonic plates moving or by volcanic activity. Most earthquakes are never felt and I have only experienced two, in my year and a half here, that were strong enough to rattle the dishware. Normally, the shaking, or more correctly the swaying, stops after 20 or 30 seconds.

While the vast majority of quakes in this country are benign, every few years a massive earthquake hits that causes damage, displacement, and sometimes death(s).

Personally, I will take the earthquakes of Costa Rica over the tornadoes of Texas – just a more scenic place for enduring a natural disaster.

6. Costa Rican's unmentionable word

In general, I do not like to generalize a society, or people. Many times a stereotype can be wrong or at the very least lead you to an incorrect assumption on the individual level.

For example, not everyone in the United States is steeped in consumerism. Not all are egotistical, and not all of the U.S. politicians are corrupt... oh, wait.

But there are certain characteristics that do shine through and are prevalent in North Americans. The same is true of the Ticos (what Costa Ricans call themselves – Tico for males and mixed company, Tica for females). The following is an example of a Tico trait that some North Americans find puzzling and annoying:

Jen and I have found a clever little diversion. When we shop at the Maxi Palí, a grocery store just outside of Grecia Centro, and we don't time the bus arrival just right (the bus comes once an hour), we walk next door to the Bar New Yorker for a beer, or a bite, to bide our time until the bus arrives.

It was here at the Bar New Yorker where I experienced first hand what many folks had warned me of ever since I moved to Costa Rica, that there is a word that is unmentionable in Costa Rica and Ticos will bend sentences any which way in order to avoid using this unmentionable word.

Before ordering my drink, I looked at the menu to see if the bar sold Bavaria Dark beer and they did. Without many craft brew choices in Costa Rica, Bavaria Dark has become my go-to beer, as it is less watery than the other national beer, Imperial, and is typically widely available.

When the waiter came around to take our order I ordered a "Bavaria Dark por favor." "Gold o Light?" came the response, the end of the sentence rising just slightly in pitch, indicating a question. Clearly the waiter did not understand what I wanted. I opened the menu again, confirmed that Bavaria Dark was indeed on it and repeated my order, this time pointing to the picture of the requested beer that was printed on the menu. Again, "Gold or Light?"

I look over to Jen for help, but instead of help, I get a look, a look that anyone else would mistake for one of pity, but to me screams, "GET THERE FASTER." And because I don't, she tells me they don't have Bavaria Dark and the waiter doesn't want to tell you "NO, you cannot have Bavaria Dark." She then tells the waiter to bring me Bavaria Gold. The waiter turns, with a smirk, and goes to place our order.

You will see the same type of response when you ask for directions. If the Tico hems and haws, crosses his arms, then tells you matter of factly where to go, there is a very large chance that he doesn't have a clue what he is talking about. But he wants to help and not disappoint so he "tries."

This can be frustrating to many North Americans, but you are here now and it is part of the culture.

Now you know no is not a word.

7. A different kind of Spanish

Growing up in Texas I learned a bit of Spanglish, a combination of Spanish and English, or at least Texan. When we moved to Costa Rica I was confident in my ability to say in Spanish: good morning (afternoon and night too), please, thank you, and you are welcome.

Imagine my surprise when, in response to me saying *gracias* (thank you), a Tico said, *con gusto*. I was expecting to hear *de nada*, which is the response one most often hears in Texas and Mexico to indicate "you are welcome" or "no problem."

Con (Mucho) Gusto, I had learned, meant "nice to meet you." Well, I ain't in Texas no more. In Costa Rica, *con gusto*, in addition to meaning "nice to meet you" is used to mean "you are welcome" or "with pleasure." I have only heard *de nada* used twice since moving here.

Another area of Spanish where I was certain I knew what I was doing consisted of greetings, like: *hola* (hello), *buenos días* (good morning), *buenas tardes* (good afternoon), *buenas noches* (good night), and *adiós* (goodbye).

Once again, I was surprised once more when I passed a Tico and in good nature said to him, *buenos días*, to which he responded, *adiós*.

This odd response of saying goodbye to me when I was saying hello reminded me of the Beatles song, *Hello, Goodbye*. Maybe more appropriately, *Help!*

For greetings in Costa Rica, this is what I have learned. You can use any of the greetings above, as they are intended/translated. In addition, you can say adiós (most likely it is actually *a Dios* (to God) as opposed to adiós (goodbye) but it sounds the same) in passing, as a replacement for any of the greetings or responses above.

Another way to consolidate greetings and responses is simply to say *buenas*, which covers all the bases: hello, goodbye, good morning, afternoon, and night.

By the way, Spanish is the official language in Costa Rica, you should learn some before visiting or moving here. The great news is the Ticos make it easy, as they are very patient with Gringos (foreigners to Costa Rica, many times singling out North Americans) as you butcher their language supplementing words with your mime skills. They like the fact that you are trying.

I would love to say I witnessed the same patience from Texans when dealing with non-English speakers.

8. Weather or not

Thanks to Costa Rica's proximity to the equator (8-12 degrees North), the country has a very consistent sunrise and sunset throughout the year. Not only is the time of sunrise and sunset consistent, it provides for a long day filled with sunshine, 12 hours of sunlight.

Give or take about 15 minutes, the sun begins each day at 5:30 a.m. and ends each day at 5:30 p.m.

While Costa Rica's weather can be all over the map, in general there are two seasons. The rainy season, also referred to as the green season (for tourists sake), or winter. It runs from May until November with the wettest month being October.

The dry season, also referred to as the high season (but not brown season), or summer, occupies the balance of the year - December through April.

One of the best tips I can give travelers who want the best bang for their buck, and who don't like crowds: visit the country during the rainy season. You will get better rates on lodging and most activities, and you will often have beaches to yourself. The reality is that the rain (normally) only lasts an hour or two each afternoon – except during October. October is the month in which you are most likely to experience non-stop rain for a day or longer.

9. The letter of the law?

Another interesting aspect for those living here is the bureaucracy's dependence on letters. While the country is wired, and has been, increasingly so, for years, the government has been slow to recognize the efficiencies that the Internet can provide.

One of the hurdles we had to overcome when we opened a bank account was to provide a letter. Letters seem to hold an exalted status when trying to get things done here. I wrote the following on my blog to commemorate our experience… or maybe to just blow off some steam:

The Letter of the Law (or the Spirit of the Letter?)
As we attempt to get things done here in Costa Rica we are beginning to see a common theme. Whether it is opening a bank account, creating an account for Internet service for our upcoming move, or canceling a service, the power of the letter in Costa Rica is impressive.

You may be confused. A letter, what is that? Well, if you remember, it is a written or typed document, on a physical piece of paper, and can state many things depending on its purpose.

Many times for Costa Rican bureaucratic purposes it just states our names, passport numbers and says that the person writing it on our behalf is our best friend and has been so for many years, despite the fact that we just met.

To open our bank account, we needed a letter of recommendation and a utility bill. We received our letter from an organization recommended by our attorney.

Unfortunately, when we were in San José to get fingerprinted (part of the residency process) and to open a bank account, we did not have a utility bill with us; it was our understanding that our attorney would "take care" of this requirement.

Well, he was unable to help with the utility bill requirement, so we went back to Grecia, and after retrieving a utility bill from our landlord, attempted to open the account at our local bank branch.

"Sorry, this utility bill is in your landlord's name; we need a letter from your landlord stating that you are renting from him. There is no need to indicate how long you have rented from him or how long your rental term is, just provide your names, passport numbers and indicate that he is your good friend and has been for many years, thank you.

Oh, one more thing, I need a letter from your attorney instructing our bank how to handle the funds, since they will be used for residency purposes, and also stating that you all are great friends."

Mind you, there is no corroboration to confirm the identity of my landlord or attorney or that what they have said in the letter is accurate or true.

Vanna, Give Me a Letter

The essence of the letter fixation in Costa Rica is this: it really doesn't matter what is in the letter, as long as you have the letter. Letters are requested to prove any number of things for any number of government entities or private companies.

The spirit of the letter is the fulfillment of bureaucracy, plain and simple. Whether it is a stamp, seal, signature, document or yet another letter, the true purpose of the required requirement is not to validate or assure but to prolong and ensure…ensure that the bureaucracy survives and thrives.

While bureaucracy here may not be so different from North America, the dependency on letters certainly is. It seems you can get business done quite easily in the States without even seeing or talking to a person. There are many other differences as well; it's one of the reasons to explore a different country to experience a different culture, a different way of doing things.

In addition to some things being completely different, some things in Costa Rica look the same, but operate a bit differently. Like shopping at various types of stores.

CHAPTER 3 – The store

There are several places that sell groceries in Costa Rica, each with their own quirks. There is the *feria*, which is a weekly, open-air farmers market that many towns host on the weekends; there is the central market, a larger permanent version of the feria typically located, you guessed it, in the center of a town; then there is the pulpería, a tiny store found in just about every community (think of a very small convenience store) that holds an incredible variety of staple items; and then there is the grocery store where you can buy just about anything you need for your household.

On the outside, grocery stores look the same as they do in the States with a huge parking lot, shopping carts strewn everywhere and small signs with specials pasted on the door as you walk through. But like everything else, there are some differences.

The naming of grocery stores is interesting in Costa Rica. A very large percentage of stores have one, or more, of the following words in the name of the store:

Mini, Maxi, Mega or Super.

Leading one to believe that each store specializes in feminine products.

In addition to the naming schemes, there are some additional differences in the grocery stores in Costa Rica when compared to those in the United States:

21

10. Lockers

The majority of the time when you first walk into a grocery store (and many department and clothing stores) you will see a set of lockers. These are there for you to store your backpack and other bags so that you don't steal from the store.

Many of the ideas that you see in Costa Rica are great. Lockers for instance, are a great idea. It is the hit or miss implementation of the great idea that can make it maddening.

The first time I walked into a grocery store I saw the lockers, but chose to ignore them, as I did not realize it was mandatory to put my backpack in one. I just walked right on by with my backpack slung over only one shoulder, like the cool kids.

BIG MISTAKE

Señor Security was on me less than 3 meters outside of the locker zone. He made a coughing noise to get my attention, and when I turned he pointed to my backpack. He made a come-hither motion with his hand and I followed.

This was my first introduction to the joys of the locker. We carry a backpack just about everywhere we go and the thing gets heavy. It is great to be able to store it somewhere, and to have it locked with a key that stays with me, while we shop.

The second time I experienced the locker culture was at a different store, but I was on the lookout – once bitten, twice shy and all that. I was looking all over the place to store my pack but didn't see one. So I went on my merry way.

BIG MISTAKE

It was not long before Señor Security was behind me and with his hand on my shoulder he turned me slightly and made a motion to follow him to the super-secret backpack storage.

Apparently, this store had cubbyholes behind a security desk and out of view from the entrance. I did not see the desk as I was focused on finding a group of lockers. And in this case, instead of a key, you get a laminated piece of paper with a number on it, so that you can claim the pack when you are done shopping.

I was a bit hesitant to store my pack this time around as I had my camera gear in my backpack, about $1,500 worth of equipment, and I did not get to lock a locker and keep the key. No, in this version of the supermarket locker you hand the bag to the security guard and he puts it in a cubbyhole and hands you a claim ticket so that you can get your bag when you are done shopping. Not to worry though, the guard has a chair there so he can sit and watch over everyone's stuff.

But what happens when an idiot gringo walks through the front door with a banned backpack slung over one shoulder, like the cool kids, and Señor Security has to jump up and chase him down to show him where his backpack goes? Who is watching the camera equipment... I mean the backpacks?

This system is a bit flawed.

The third time (yes there was a third time) there were lockers, but they were all shut and had no keys sticking out. I gave a dubious look to Señor Security, he just shrugged and he waved me on.

11. Bagging tip

In many stores, you will bag your own groceries or the cashier will do it for you. Occasionally, you will be at a grocery store where there is a bagger who seems to be out of place. He (or she - but really, it's going to be a he) is young, real young, and is not dressed in the uniform of the store.

This guy is a freelancer, a motivated entrepreneur who is working solely for tips. He is too young to work for the store – or they don't want to hire him – but he will bag your groceries with zeal. We like to tip this guy. You do what you want.

When the cashier acts as the bagger, many times, as he or she rings up the items, they will use a triangular shaped spinning device that has racks holding two bags, side by side. This allows the cashier to fill two bags, spin the contraption and fill two additional bags, then spin, and so on. Beware; it is easy to miss a bag that has your groceries in it because it is hidden from your view. I have chased down patrons twice now, who have left their (paid for) items in the spinner.

12. Size doesn't matter

Like many North Americans, I too have been brainwashed into the bulk mentality. Why buy one when you can get six cheaper? Shopping in the U.S. taught us that to be frugal we needed to buy in bulk. Sam's Club and Costco were our friends.

Here in Costa Rica it can be a bit different. Bulk items are available, but, sometimes you will actually pay *more* for the item in bulk or large size than if you bought the smaller size or multiple individual packages.

Here is a recent example – honest to god – a 250 gram bag of 1820 coffee (a damn good coffee, by the way) was ₡1250 or ₡5 per gram and that same coffee in the KILO size (4 times the size for those metrically challenged) was ₡5,300, or ₡5.3 per gram.

Another example is butter. Many times it is cheaper to buy four individual sticks of butter than to buy the four-pack box of butter.

Don't ask me why.

It does not always happen that prices for larger sizes cost more, but it happens enough to watch out for it.

Bigger is not necessarily better.

13. Caja Rápida (life in the fast lane?)

This term is both a misnomer as well as an oxymoron.

Caja is the Spanish term for, among other things, cashier, and Rápida is the Spanish term for quick or fast.

So, Caja + Rápida = The Fast Lane.

To be clear, nothing having to do with a cashier in Costa Rica is fast. There are many things that may slow you down: a suspicious colón, a barcode that is not in the system, a conversation the cashier is having or, especially in the case of the Caja Rápida line, a customer with about 200 items in his shopping cart.

In the States, the "Express Lane" almost always has a sign dictating the maximum number of items you can have in order to participate in the express'ness of the lane. There is no such precision for the Caja Rápida lane in many Costa Rican stores.

The lane acts much as the stop sign in Costa Rica – merely a suggestion - a suggestion that maybe you should limit the number of items in your cart; a suggestion that no one follows and a suggestion that makes the sign designating the registers' quickness unnecessary. We are learning that in Costa Rica, things take more time, not just at the grocery store, but in just about everything we do. It is ok. Slow down.

Relax. Pura Vida.

14. Load phone/pay bills

One of the conveniences that you find in Costa Rica is the ability to pay bills and charge your phone minutes at the grocery store and at many kiosk locations in each town.

For cell phones, until you have residency status and obtain your Cedula, you can only have a pay-as-you-go cell phone plan. These plans require you to reload your phone shortly before or when you run out of minutes, to continue service. We load 2,000 colones at a time (about $4) and this lasts us about a month. Granted, we do not yap on the phone too much. Loading the phone this way includes data as well so that you can have Internet access in a non-Wi-Fi area.

Typically, you load your phone through the cashier by providing your phone number, phone company (MoviStar, Claro, or Kolbi) and how much money you wish to load.

It can be frustrating to be in a grocery line behind someone who only has one item only to see them throw down four phone cards to refill at the end of the transaction – in the Caja Rápida line no doubt. It can take a minute or two to load each card.

Something to keep an eye out for are bonus promotions. We have our cell service through MoviStar and often get texts that inform us that we can get double minutes, or more, for refilling on certain days with a minimum amount of colones loaded. Obviously we refill our phones on those days.

For bill payment, many stores have an area in front of the store specifically for bills. You can pay your Internet/cable, electric, and water bills and perform other financial transactions. In a lot of areas each *barrio* or neighborhood has its own water supply and company. In cases such as this the water bill must be paid locally, usually at a pulpería in the neighborhood.

15. Expensive items

As a general rule, anything that has to be imported into Costa Rica is expensive, sometimes very expensive, compared to prices in the States. For those who move here and love the comforts of home, this can be a budget buster. In general the following items cost two to three times more in Costa Rica than in the U.S.:

Cheese

Razors

Shaving Cream

Ice Chests/Coolers

Sunscreen

All Varieties of Nuts

One way to spot these items quickly is to look for the locked glass cases in the stores. They will typically be filled with rows and rows of sunscreen and shaving products.

The flipside of the cost coin is that if you love fruits and vegetables you can buy them very cheaply. And if you have a green thumb and a bit of land you can grow your own.

16. Tang is a thing

An oddity you will see in many grocery stores in Costa Rica is the Tang Aisle. Ok, so maybe it is not an entire aisle but man, Costa Ricans love their Tang. There are rows and rows of the powdery drink in many flavors. I guess they sell a lot of it, although I never see anyone buying it.

17. Spanish names for grocery items

My wife likes to bake, and she is very good at it (it's why I hike so much). When we first moved here she had a hard time finding the supplies she needed.

Sometimes the items were not in a logical place, to her North American way of thinking, and sometimes the name of the item or its packaging was completely different than she was used to.

With that in mind, here are some common ingredients and their Spanish names and product differences, if any, to the U.S. equivalent:

Sour Cream: Natilla in Costa Rica– Much more liquid-y than its U.S. equivalent. It is not really sour cream, but it is the closest thing Costa Rica has – it is more like crème fraiche but a hint of sour taste. In other Latin American countries (Cuba, Mexico, Peru, etc.) natilla is the same consistency but sweet.

Cream Cheese: Queso Crema – Very similar to cream cheese in the States except a bit softer.

Buttermilk: Leche Agria (translates to Sour Milk) – Similar to that which is available in the U.S. but harder to find.

You can make your own buttermilk by adding 1 tablespoon of white vinegar or lemon juice to 1 cup of at least 2% milk. Stir and let sit for 5 minutes and you have buttermilk.

Sugar: Azúcar – Product is the same as in the U.S.

Salt: Sal – Product is the same as in the U.S.

Yeast: Levadura – Product is the same as in the U.S.

Basil: Albahaca.

Parsley: Perejil.

Rosemary: Romero.

Even though there are differences in these staple items, they are similar enough to be able to complete most recipes.

18. Be aware of freebies

Something that amuses me here are the "Gratis" specials often found in grocery stores.

The deals are amusing for three reasons:

First, the free item is usually just attached to the main item with packing tape with a "Gratis" sticker slapped over the tape. This would never happen in the U.S., where much thought and money goes into advertising. The freebee there would have its own packaging and it would look like the two items went together and not just stuck together as an afterthought.

Secondly, the promotional item, many times, is not at all related to the main product. I have seen a Glade air-freshener attached to roach spray (I guess that does make scents). Another example seen recently was a package of Ritz crackers taped to a box of cereal.

There may be some method to the madness of these promotions, but to me it appears that the stores are just trying to get rid of an extraneous product by taping it to another product that they are trying to move.

Finally, the last oddity of this freebee practice is that sometimes, it ain't free. What I mean is, if you brought the product that is wrapped with a free gift up to the register along with the same product without the free product, the one with the extra item might be more expensive.

Related to this last item is the hilarious practice I have seen where a half-sheet of paper announcing a promotional item is taped over the original price sticker attached to the shelf. When you lift up the half-sheet and look at the original price, it is the same as the promotional price.

19. Cash handling oddness

There are some types of stores that handle each transaction in a peculiar way.

First up the butcher. At the butcher at the farmers market we have witnessed the following system: you order your beef, chicken or fish, the butcher wraps it up and sets it aside. Then he will grasp a plastic bowl and thrust it at you. You place your money into the bowl and then he hands the bowl to a cashier.

I imagine this is so that the butcher's latex gloved-hand does not come into contact with the money or the germs on it. I guess there are no germs on the bowl.

Next up is the cash handling at some hardware stores. It should be mentioned first that at many *ferreterías* (hardware stores) you do not have access to all (or any) of the items available for sale. In order to purchase, or even look at a product, you have to speak (yes, in Spanish) to an employee. They will then go get what they think you described from rows of products behind them, or worse, call another associate and describe what he thinks you are looking for (ever play the telephone game?). After awhile you will get to see what they came up with and after some back and forth you will get what you came for, maybe.

If that wasn't inefficient enough, when it is time to pay, you have a two-step process to check out. First the employee who helped you will itemize a ticket and package your items. He will then hand you the inventory list and you will walk to the other side of the store to the cashier to complete the financial part of your transaction. The cashier rings you up; you pay. The cashier then stamps your receipt and you walk back across the store to the man who is patiently awaiting your return. After scrutinizing the stamp, he smiles and gives you your purchased items while you walk away wondering what just happened.

I am not sure the reason for handling cash this way, and it is not just at hardware stores. Other types of retail outlets have a similar system. It might be to thwart theft by employees or just to create more work for the employees. Whatever the reason, you now know what to expect.

20. Stamps and staples

In addition to the checkout procedure, you can see from the example above, stores in Costa Rica love to stamp receipts. Actually, it is not just stores; just about every place you do business (except the grocery store) involves stamping your receipt.

In most retail stores, when you purchase something, after the item is bagged it will then be tagged. First they will place your purchase in an appropriately sized bag, then fold over the top and put a couple of staples in (sometimes tape as well), then they will stamp your receipt and staple it to the bag. Once again, I believe this is to reduce theft – even though if you walk into a different store with your stamped receipt and stapled package, you are most likely going to be requested to place it in a locker.

21. Beer and wine and liquor

Wine, beer and liquor can be bought at most grocery stores. Beer here, even the national brands, is expensive compared to the U.S. A six-pack of Imperial will run you about 4,000 colones ($8) - this for a beer on par with Miller or Bud. Ouch.

Some deals can be had in the wine department. There are box wines from Chile and Argentina that are not bad and run 2,000 – 3,500 colones per liter ($4 - $7). Also, if you are paying attention you can pick up some really yummy bottles for under $10.

Most stores that have beer and wine also have liquor. Brands that you know and love from the U.S. are going to be more expensive here than in the States. If you are a bourbon drinker, like me, you are going to have a hard time finding anything at all. The same holds true for tequila. Vodka and rum drinkers, you guys are covered pretty well with the Nicaraguan brand of rum Flor de Caña being a favorite both for price and taste. For a bargain try the local firewater called *guaro*, the most well known brand being Cacique. Use it in any drink where you would use vodka.

The best deal, by far, is found by visiting the duty free store at SJO as you enter the country. You are allowed 5 liters per passenger and the price is normally much better than in the States or at a store here. One of the best deals is Stolichnaya vodka; a liter will cost just $10 compared to about $18 in the U.S.

22. Free produce número uno

One trick I have learned at the local farmers market is to go on the last day, towards the time that it is shutting down.

Here in Grecia that is Saturday around noon.

When you go at this time the selection will not be as great, as many farmers will already have left, or will have sold much of their produce.

The trade off is that you will often get up to twice as much produce for your money. You will pick out three avocados and the farmer will add another two or three to your bag. This is not guaranteed but it happens enough to warrant consideration as a strategy.

23. Free produce número dos

Another way I get free fresh produce (primarily fruits) is to walk farm roads the mornings of the feria. Farm roads are typically bumpy and fruit laden trucks will often spill fruit destined for the feria onto the road.

It is also a good idea to make friends with the landowners along your hiking route. Fruit trees are plentiful and most owners have an excess of fruits and are happy to give them to you.

Exercise and free food: what could be better?

24. Nap time

Many stores like electronic stores, clothing stores and appliance stores (typically not the grocery store, but maybe the pulpería) close for an hour or two around lunchtime. It may be inconvenient but, once again, knowing is half the battle.

CHAPTER 4 – The restroom

Things that happen in the bathroom can always be a source of humor (or horror). This is especially true in Costa Rica, or I imagine any foreign country.

The reality is that you ARE in a foreign place and the easiest of things can be complicated simply because you do not know what to expect – or don't expect what you get.

Add to that the potential of being caught in an embarrassing situation – with your pants down, so to speak – and it is necessary for me to share my newfound tips regarding the *necessary room.*

I have already admitted that I am not a well-traveled person. That being said, here are the things about the bathroom, restroom, lavatory, etc… here in Costa Rica that I wish I had known before I moved here.

25. Doing the do

The first night of our due diligence trip to Costa Rica in 2012 was spent at a Bed & Breakfast in Grecia. The place was a house converted into a B&B and each of the two rooms downstairs shared a bathroom.

I have already mentioned the sheltered life I had led up to this point. This was only the second time I had stayed somewhere with a shared bathroom and I am one who likes to keep my private business private.

I was keeping an eye on the restroom because I had to go, but I didn't want anyone to know. Finally, with the coast clear, I made my way to the bathroom and took care of business.

As I finished I looked across to the wall facing me, and there at eye level was a sign that read, "Do not put toilet paper in the toilet."

I thought, surely it couldn't mean what it said, and after assuring myself it was ok, I flushed the toilet paper instead of following the arrow underneath the sign to the sealed garbage can.

Later, I managed to cleverly bring this topic up to the Inn Keeper. He informed me that yes, I read the sign right and no, it was not ok to flush the paper down the toilet. Instead, used toilet paper should be placed in the provided garbage can.

Not all toilets in Costa Rica are like this. I have been told that the reason for not flushing the paper is that the size of the pipes used in the plumbing is too small for today's paper or the water pressure is inadequate. Many toilets have been updated to be able to accommodate the triple ply, but there are still plenty of restrooms throughout the country that insist on the no-paper-in-the-toilet policy.

The moral of the story is, if you see a sign telling you not to flush the toilet paper – don't. As odd as it sounds, just throw it in the sealed garbage can that is provided.

26. BYO-TP

A correlating tip to the one above is that some restrooms will be "out" of toilet paper. It may be because it is expensive or that they forgot to stock it. For whatever reason it behooves you to bring a couple of squares along wherever you go.

Here is a recent, real life example:

> A couple of weeks ago we took a road trip down to Sierpe, a river town on the Osa peninsula. We stopped at several motels to find the best deal and settled on one just outside the center of town for a very reasonable $45 a night, breakfast included.
>
> Over the 3 days we were there we whittled the half roll of toilet paper that was provided in the room down to nothing. So I asked the manager for another roll. He came back with an opened package of napkins, and with a sheepish grin said, "This is all we have."
>
> This is not a fluke event. I have seen the same thing over and over again at public restrooms throughout the country. Be prepared.

27. Pay-to-play

If you are out and about and need to go, another thing to be aware of is that sometimes a restroom will be available but you will need to pay.

The cost is always more expensive to sit than to stand, and I have seen it range from ₡100 to ₡500. The most expensive (₡500) was seen at a deserted beach – deserted except for a bathroom attendant and us.

The majority of the time, the pay-to-play places are in busy public locations such as the bus terminal or a central market.

28. Center console

One brilliant idea that is implemented by many Costa Rican restrooms is the central wash area. Instead of having two or three sinks and mirrors in each of the men and ladies' restrooms, there is a common area between the two doors for all to use.

This area is usually behind a door or other visible barrier. This can cause confusion or concern. If you are paranoid, like me, of entering the wrong gender's restroom, then this set-up can cause a brief moment of panic, as you just don't know if you are in the right place.

Luckily, in Costa Rica (once you get to the center console area) the doors are labeled simply, "Damas" or "Mujeres" for the women and "Cabelleros" or "Hombres" for the men.

None of the clever craziness, seen mainly in U.S. themed restaurants, that causes so much worry for people such as me. When I need to go, I really don't want the, albeit brief, indecision of deciding if I am a Hen or a Rooster, a Bloke or a Sheila, a Stand-Up or a Sit-Down, or worst yet, a Have or a Have Not.

Costa Rica's restroom signage is clear and straightforward, whew.

29. Open range

This tip is for the men. Some restrooms here have no main door. There may be a partial wall hiding an open door frame, or saloon doors that are open on the bottom and top, or just a doorframe for you to walk into. AND many restrooms have their urinals right when you walk through that opening. The result – you can be seen while you do your stand-up business.

These types of restrooms are mostly in bars, but I have seen them in restaurants as well. They can be a bit unnerving to use, especially when there is only room for one person and there is a line.

30. That's what pants are for

Similar to the "no toilet paper" issue is the fact that many public restrooms do not have an air hand dryer or paper towels for you to use after you have washed your hands.

It is a great way to see who doesn't wash their hands – if they are not shaking their hands in the air or wiping

them on their clothes when they exit the restroom, well
ewwww.

31. Shocking shower

No doubt you have heard of a suicide shower, but if you
have never seen one, the first time you do, it will shock
you. Just to see wires routed to a showerhead will give
most of you shivers.

Yes, electricity is run to a showerhead, ignoring that bit
of wisdom to not mix water and electricity. The
electricity hits a heating element in the showerhead and
heats the water "on demand" – a much more palatable
description than "suicide shower" and the one that is
typically used.

The reality is, the suicide shower is widely used
throughout Central America and I have never heard of
an accident, but still.

32. Getting into hot water

Electricity can be expensive in Costa Rica. In fact,
electrical costs are tiered and after hitting a certain level
of usage the rate per kilowatt increases, sometimes
significantly.

Because of this, electrical use is monitored heavily by
cost conscience Ticos and Gringos. As a result, many

homes do not have a hot water heater, hence the suicide shower.

This also means no hot water in the kitchen – an oddity for those from North America. In fact, there is dish soap made specifically for use with cold water (Axion is the brand). The hot water problem is sometimes solved by having a hose or reservoir on the roof of a home that can be heated by the sun to provide warm, if not hot, water.

Then again, some homes just go without hot water; for those on a budget, these homes typically are the least expensive to lease.

33. Lights out

For the final tip in this section I would suggest you install a flashlight app on your cell phone. In the similar vein of not stocking enough toilet paper, some public restrooms will have a light bulb that needs to be replaced.

So you have to go but there is no light in the restroom. I have experienced this scenario twice now and let's just say the second time was less stressful as I was prepared with the light app on my phone.

CHAPTER 5 – The restaurant

Eating out can be frustrating for someone visiting Costa Rica or for someone who is newly expatriated, especially if he is accustomed to the restaurant experiences typically found in the United States.

Service, or what you might consider lack of service, will be the most noticeable difference. "Turning" a table is not a concern here and a meal can easily take twice as long as you are accustomed to and wait staff do not have the, "he took a sip, I better go refill his glass" mentality. In fact it is almost the exact opposite. For example, your empty beer bottle will go unnoticed until you mention you would like another beer, and then it still might take 10 minutes to get it. Life moves at a slower pace and so does service.

If it really drives you crazy, order two beers at a time. Beer is frequently served with a glass of ice (yes, a glass of ice) so you know the second one can still be enjoyed cold.   The dining experience in tourists' towns will be better, but probably still not the service level you remember from home.

Relax. Knowing what to expect is half the battle. The other half is to embrace the *Pura Vida* attitude and enjoy the slower pace. Constantly remind yourself - this is not your country.

34. Dig in

From an early age those who were taught manners were taught to wait to eat until everyone at the table was served. This is a great rule to follow in the States where most restaurants time meals to all come out at the same time.

In Costa Rica I have created a new rule: When someone's food comes out, he should start eating – if he wants to eat it hot, that is. The reality is that it may be a long time before the next person receives his meal.

Kind of like fighting over a tab when a friend wants to buy, waiting for everyone to be brought their meal is an ingrained habit, but a useless one in Costa Rica. When we tell guests who get their food first to please start, they don't – they feel an understandable obligation to wait. Then we insist and still they wait. Our food comes out 15 minutes later and they eat cold food.

Told you so, and yes, you can buy my lunch.

35. Pricing doesn't always make sense

We have a favorite *soda* (a small, family owned, Tico-style restaurant) that we go to where you can really get a great deal. For $6 you can get a *casado* (a typical Costa Rican dish) that is piled with rice, beans, fresh avocado, potatoes, grilled chicken breast, all topped with a fried egg.

Or, for the same price, at the same restaurant, you can get a small bowl of black bean dip served with a few chips.

Price and quantity, or even quality, do not always correlate. Typically, if you order the typical Costa Rican dishes, a casado, *arroz con something* (rice with chicken, beef, pork, or fish), or *gallo pinto* (rice and beans, served with tortillas and sometimes eggs or a meat), you will get the best deals.

36. Beer, the cheapest drink on the menu

Surprisingly, a Costa Rican national beer, like Imperial or Baveria may be the least expensive drink on the menu. In our medium sized farming town in the Central Valley an Imperial at a restaurant costs about $2. You would most likely pay more in a tourist area or at a beach.

Many times beer is served *con hielo* or with a glass of ice, which is really great as ice-chest cold bottles are a rarity. The beer can also be served as a *michelada*. In Costa Rica a michelada is a bottle of beer served alongside a salt rimmed glass filled about a quarter of the way up with lime juice; add the ice and pour in the beer and you have a tasty treat. It is my favorite way to liven up the relatively bland beers of Costa Rica.

In Mexico and other Latin American countries the michelada is more like a Bloody Mary made with beer instead of vodka. It can be served with a variety of tomato and Clamato juices as well as peppers or other items - this in addition to the aforementioned salt-rimmed glass, lime juice, ice, and beer.

A soft drink will cost about the same, or more, as a beer and it will most likely come in a plastic or glass bottle. Fountain drinks and tap beer alike are less common in Costa Rica than their bottled counterparts.

37. Other typical beverages

In addition to beer and soft drinks, restaurants carry a few other types of beverages:

Té Frío – Costa Rica's version of iced tea, sometimes served over ice and sometimes the ice is blended so that the drink is slushy (and yummy).

Another favorite is a fresco or refresco. These fruit drinks are made by blending ice, fruit, with either water (*en agua*), or milk (*en leche*).

Common fruits used in frescos are: *piña* (pineapple), *mora* (tastes like a tart blackberry), *mango* (hey, you probably know this one) and *guanábana* (soursop fruit).

38. Food with a view

There is a chain of restaurants here that all have the word *mirador* in the name. Ok, it is not really a chain, but the word is used a lot in restaurant names. If a restaurant does have that word in it, it means that there is an overlook or a view. Some of my favorite dining experiences here have been at a restaurant with a mirador.

Many times a mediocre food experience can be made memorable with the addition of dining al fresco and having a wonderful view.

39. Check it out

In the States when your meal is complete, after you have declined (or indulged in) dessert, the server brings the bill. You pay. They bring change or you sign. You leave.

In Costa Rica, you can ask for *la cuenta por favor* (the bill please), and you may wait for a very long time to receive it. Most places, I have found, expect you to go to a central counter or bar, where there is a cash register, to pay as opposed to a waiter bringing the bill to your table.

As you eat, observe what others are doing at the end of their meal and follow suit, because it is not just at the sodas where you pay at the counter. We have paid this way at a very nice steak house as well – after waiting about 30 minutes for the waiter to bring the bill.

The good news about paying this way is that you will never be rushed. In fact the only time I have felt rushed was when our group of six unknowingly walked into a restaurant 15 minutes before they closed.

We were served a full meal, declined dessert and settled in to talking when all of a sudden lights started turning off. I talked with the manager and he explained the situation, I apologized and our group moved on to another location to continue our conversation. This was another example of the indirect, not wanting to say "no" way that Ticos communicate.

40. To tip or not to tip

To tip or not tip – that truly is a question. Here is the deal: the restaurant bill (typically) has an automatic 10% gratuity added. This 10% is supposed to go to the server for his or her work.

There are two different viewpoints on tipping:

The non-tipper justifies not tipping because, HELLO, there is already a tip on the bill and the Ticos don't tip. This person reasons that if Gringos tip extra they will receive preferential treatment in the service depart compared to the Tico who does not tip extra.

The other viewpoint is that the included 10% won't make it into the server's pocket, plus it is only 10% and not the 15 – 20% North Americans typically leave, and the Ticos are not making much anyway.

I will leave it at that; my tip being to inform you that there is a debate about tipping, do what you think is right.

41. A memorable meal

An oddity of eating out in Costa Rica is that, more times than not, you will need to recount the items you purchased for your meal when you pay the bill.

I don't know why this is a "thing," but rest assured, it is. The waiter writes down your order and when the food comes out it is normally correct, but when you go to pay there is a disconnect. The waiter will look at you and may point to where he wrote down your order, waiting for you to list the items you consumed. Most establishments do not have Point of Sale registers and still depend on a manual system… and your memory.

The good news is it helps your Spanish, at least in regards to foods – which are of course the first Spanish words you should learn after learning the words for, please, thank you, and I am sorry.

42. Restaurant Spanish

Sin means without: example: sin cebollas – without onions

How do you like your steak?
rojo – rare
medio rojo – medium rare
medio – medium
tres cuartos – medium well
bien cocida – well done

Things on la mesa (the table)
la cuchara – spoon
el cuchillo – knife
el tenedor – fork
el vaso – glass
la servilleta – napkin

Spice it up
el salero – salt shaker
el pimentero – pepper shaker
salsa picante or salsa chile – hot sauce

Other important things
el pan – bread
el postre – dessert
la bebida – drink

43. Scheduling conflicts

One of the things you will notice, mainly if you are in a non-tourist area is that restaurants keep strange hours and are closed on strange days. I say strange because each restaurant is different and there is seemingly no rhyme or reason to the schedule.

Most restaurants post a schedule of days and hours, but this doesn't mean they will be open during this time. We have a group of about 10 eateries that we like in the town in which we live, Grecia. We know if it is Monday that at least 3 of them will be closed, and if it is Tuesday 4 of them will be closed, and it could be more depending on what is going on in the lives of the owners.

Things like this tend to mess with the North American mind. We USA'ians lean towards wanting what we want... NOW!

Well, guess what? You are in Costa Rica; it is a different country and it operates differently.

Relax, you will not go hungry.

CHAPTER 6 – The bank

There is no way around it; banks are a necessary part of
life. It is not feasible, here or anywhere, to hide
thousands of dollars under your mattress. Additionally, if
you are in Costa Rica, and all your money is in U.S.
dollars, you will eventually need to convert the dollars to
Costa Rican colones.

The banks in Costa Rica look similar to and perform the
same basic functions as their counterparts in the U.S.,
but they do it a bit differently. Just entering the bank
here can be a daunting task to the uninitiated, not to
mention trying to complete a transaction. If you have
not been to a bank in Costa Rica you may be surprised
by the differences.

Here are a few of the things we have experienced:

44. Getting into Fort Knox

In the United States, entering a bank is like walking into
any other type of building - you open the door and walk
in. The process of entering a bank in Costa Rica can be a
little more arduous.

The first thing you will notice is that security at Costa
Rican banks is taken very seriously. Before you are
allowed in, you have to navigate what I call the "isolation
booth." This is a glass-enclosed box that you enter so
that a guard can check you out.

First, you press a button that opens the first of two sliding glass doors. When you enter, the door closes behind you, cocooning you in a glass box. As you stand there, unsure of what to do next, a security guard looks you over. If you have a backpack or a purse, you open it to show the guard that there is nothing dangerous in the bag - never mind that you only show him one of the ten pockets of your bag.

Finally, when the guard is confident that you are not going to rob the bank with the contents of your backpack, he opens the door that is in front of you and allows you to enter the main area of the bank.

This whole process doesn't take very long, but it can be unnerving the first time it is experienced. It's not just having a guard with a gun staring you down that is stressful. Sometimes the straightforward procedure is made a bit awkward because the guard is also managing the isolation booth designated for the people exiting the bank as well as the one for those entering. Or he is helping some unaware Gringo with the computerized queuing machine.

45. Take a number please

The next hurdle that stands between you and a teller is navigating the ticketing system. In order to be in the queue for a teller you must take a number, similar to how you get your salami at the deli counter.

There are two systems that I have seen being used in various banks. The first is the easiest. You take a paper number from one of two different dispensers based on which line you need. One dispenser is for the normal teller and one is for the sit-down teller. The sit-down teller, or "personal banker", helps with opening accounts and other more complicated transactions.

The second method of obtaining your number and the one that always causes me to pull the security guard away from isolation booth duty is computerized, and hence, more complicated. You must scroll through multiple screens, which are in Spanish (naturally) and choose all the correct options for your situation. I imagine as my Spanish gets better, so will my ability to get the ticket from the computer without assistance.

46. Bingo

Once you receive your ticket you are one step closer to getting to the point where you can begin your transaction. Now you wait… and wait. Seriously, waiting is part of the game here - not just at the bank, but also everywhere.

You wait in a large area with rows and rows of chairs, maybe 50 of them, and many of them will be occupied.

There is a television or other system displaying a letter and a number combination. The letter corresponds to a specific teller window and the number is your place in the pecking order.

When the letter and number on the TV screen matches what is on your ticket… BINGO, you are up.

47. Then again

Those first three tips are more or less true for Costa Rica's state owned banks: Banco Nacional, Banco de Costa Rica and Banco Créditto Agrícola de Cartago, and a special-charter bank called Banco Popular. If you want a real treat and a taste of home go to a private bank such as ScotiaBank as, many times, they do not have the same security measures in place nor such long lines.

48. Stupid Gringo

There are some things that are allowed in banks in the U.S. that are not tolerated in Costa Rica, and they make a ton of sense to me:

- You cannot wear sunglasses in the bank.

- You cannot wear a baseball cap or any other type of hat in the bank. Leave your Indiana Jones hat at home, or put it in your backpack and show it to security when you are in the isolation booth.

- If you need moral support from your spouse, because you are nervous about the transaction, you better get it before you hit BINGO and head to the teller – only one person at the teller at a time, por favor.

- Do not talk or text on your cell phone. YEAH, someone finally gets it.

Doing any of these things will make a bank employee come over and talk with you while pointing at your head, eyes or hand because he knows you don't understand what he is saying. Stupid Gringo.

49. Converting to Costa Rican

Most likely one of the reasons you will be using the bank is to convert your U.S. dollars into Costa Rican colones. Luckily for you, the exchange rate (which has been relatively consistent over the past ten years) is, roughly, 500 colones to one dollar.

This makes the math of converting, even for the numerically challenged, relatively easy. All you have to do is remove the last three digits from the colones amount and multiply whatever is left by two.

For example, to figure the dollar equivalent for something that costs 10,000 colones, you would remove the last 3 digits (000) leaving you with 10. Take 10 and multiply times 2 to end up with $20. So, 10,000 colones is $20.

When converting colones to dollars, it is always best to convert your money at a bank as they will have the best rate. The very worst place to convert your money (aside from the guy on the street who will, more than likely, take the money and run) is at the airport. The currency companies that are at the airport offer the least favorable exchange rate. It's like playing the slot machines at the airport in Vegas – just don't do it.

The exchange rate does fluctuate. Currently it is at 530 colones to the dollar, and so this method is useful only as an estimate.

Exchanging dollars for colones at a bank is easy, even if you have no Spanish. At a minimum, place the money you want exchanged on the counter, point at it and say *colones, por favor*. The teller will understand that you have not taken the time to learn any Spanish and will smile and convert your money.

Before they convert the cash, the bank employee will ask to see your passport. If you are exchanging a large amount, say over a couple of hundred dollars, they may make a copy of your passport.

At the end of the transaction you will be presented with a receipt; it will show a break down of the amount of dollars you started with, the exchange rate, and the amount of colones you now have in your possession. You will be handed a pen so you can sign the receipt, then you will be handed a clean receipt of your transaction to keep for your records.

50. Colón(ize)

The Costa Rican unit of money, the colón ("colones" plural) pays homage to that serial colonizer Cristóbal Colón aka Christopher Columbus. Not only did Costa Rica name their money after ole Chris they also named a city in the Central Valley after him, Ciudad Colón.

51. Costa Rican denominations

The colón, like U.S. currency, is represented both in coin and paper varieties in a wide range of denominations.

The coins come in the following denominations: ₡5, ₡10, ₡25, ₡50, ₡100 and ₡500, with each coin varying in size - the larger the coin, the greater the value - unlike the craziness with the U.S. dime.

The most common examples of the ₡5 and ₡10 coins are made of aluminum and are reminiscent of a board game's play money. They are light and will float on water, but otherwise they are relatively useless, having a value of about 1 cent and 2 cents respectively.

All the other coins are made of a gold colored metal that is much heavier and less toy-like. The largest coin is the ₡500 coin and it is about the size of a U.S. silver dollar and is, roughly, equivalent in value to the same.

The best thing about Costa Rican coins? They work great for playing poker if poker-chips are not available.

The paper versions of colones come in the following denominations: ₡1,000, ₡2,000, ₡5,000, ₡10,000, ₡20,000 and the recently released ₡50,000 note.

There is nothing quite like the feeling you have the first time you walk up to an ATM and type in a huge number, like 200,000, for the amount of colones to withdraw. The first time I did it, I recalculated in my head at least three times the conversion of $400 to ₡200,000, and still there was a long pause, after typing 200,000, before I hit enter.

Counterfeiting is apparently a problem in Costa Rica and store clerks are ever vigilant in sniffing out the bogus bucks. You will almost always see them hold the bill up to the light or run a fingernail over the bill to determine if it is real.

One last thing about the colón, when the number is written down, Tico scribes (as well as scribes in other countries) will sometimes use a comma as the decimal point where us USA'ians would use a point. For example what a North American would write as ₡1,000.50, a Costa Rican *might* write it as ₡1.000,50 – confusing the hell out of the unaware.

Now you know.

52. It's interesting

Banks in Costa Rica pay a very favorable interest rate on CD's. Currently, a one-year CD pays out right around 6%. Pretty incredible when compared to a CD in a U.S. bank account. You have to take into consideration inflation when considering whether or not investing using the local currency is right for you.

You can get even better rates if you bank at one of the credit unions. Rates orbiting the 12% mark for a 5-year commitment are not unheard of. You must be a resident to open an account at a credit union and these rates are good for investments made with colones, and please remember: the value of the colón to the dollar fluctuates.

The flipside of the interest coin is that those who are seeking credit are going to pay through the nose – sometimes well over 20% for those unfortunate souls who do not have cash on hand.

53. Here's the problem

I know – you can't wait to get your money over here and invest it, right? Well, you are going to have to – wait, that is. The U.S. doesn't want you to move your money away so they are cracking down on the reporting necessary both for the individuals and the banks. On top of this, Costa Rican banks are not the most efficient paper pushers out there.

What this means for you, the average Joe or Jill, is that you cannot open a bank account in Costa Rica... unless:

> You have residency as verified by possession of a Cedula

> > or

> You own property in Costa Rica

> > or

> You have registered a Costa Rican Corporation

I have heard stories of people opening bank accounts without fitting one of the above criteria. I also know someone who won $10,000 from a lottery scratch-off ticket.

To give you an example of opening an account without having any of the above qualifications, I will tell you our tale of opening an account.

All said, it took us five trips to the bank in order to open an account. Granted, we were trying to wire into the country a relatively large sum of money, enough to comply with the Rentista residency requirement.

> **First Attempt** – Our attorney had assured us that opening an account was "no hay problema" as he had 15 years of experience dealing with Banco National (the bank he recommended) and they knew how to set up the account with a CD that would distribute the requisite amount of money each month for our residency type.
>
> After going through the security rigmarole, we waited a few minutes to see a personal banker. When our turn came our translator began talking with the teller in Spanish, letting her know the type of account we needed to open. He explained to her that we had our residency in process, also called having your expediente number (folio number). Our attorney had insisted that this was all the bank would need to open our account.
>
> Our personal banker disagreed and requested that we bring in a utility bill with our address on it. We explained that we were renting and the utility bill would be in our landlord's name. "No hay problema."

We left the bank to hunt for a utility bill.

Second Attempt – With our utility bill in hand, and a spring in our step, we took our attorney's advice and headed to the local Grecia branch of Banco National to avoid going all the way to San José.

We brought a Tica friend with us to translate.

Apparently, the Grecia branch does not typically set up accounts to fulfill residency requirements and so the personal banker requested a detailed letter from our attorney specifying how to set up the account. In addition, the personal banker requested three additional letters from various sources for various reasons.

He did not care that we had a utility bill.

Back to San José.

Third Attempt – We headed back to San José a couple of weeks later to finally get our account opened. We once again walked with our translator into the bank and were told that the utility letter would not work as it was in the name of a corporation.

Instead, our personal banker told us that what they really needed was a letter from our brokerage account administrator in the States, informing the bank that we have funds available to transfer and identifying the source of these funds.

I verified that if we did indeed bring the letter that the bank was now requesting, there would be "no hay problema" the next time we returned.

We were told it would be so.

Fourth Attempt – We arrived by bus in San José and met with our translator at the attorney's office. We walked the now familiar path to Banco National and took our ticket.

We successfully presented the requested letter from the legal department of the firm where our brokerage account was and the banker gave us a smile.

I started to feel good.

She asked us for our passports so she could make a copy of them for her records and as she was perusing our passport her smile slowly turned upside down.

Uh, oh.

On this day we were unable to open our account because our tourist visa had expired. It didn't seem to matter that our residency paperwork was in process and that we had been issued our expediency numbers and that we were no longer required by law to leave the country every 90 days to renew the visa.

They say the definition of insanity is doing the same thing time and time again but expecting a different result.

With this in mind, we walked with our translator down the street to ScotiaBank. There was no security hurdle and no need to take a number. We checked in with the information desk and they had us take a seat.

A few minutes later a personal banker came out and greeted us with a smile and a handshake. His English was better than our Spanish and we were able to dismiss our translator.

After reviewing the details of what we were trying to accomplish he detailed what we would need to open an account with Scotia.

I deflated.

Apparently, this time we needed a utility bill with our name and address on it. I had a sense of déjà vu and dread. The only utility that was in our name was our Internet account and we asked if this would work and the answer was "no hay problema."

The second item we needed was our previous year's tax return.

Seriously?

Yes, seriously.

It seemed as though we had been in this exact situation before, but our banker insisted that if we complied with these requirements we would be able to open the account.

He also explained that normally to open an account, a bank patron needed to be either a resident, own property, or own a corporation. With the requested documentation and our paperwork showing that our residency was in process, he said that ScotiaBank was willing to make an exception.

Fingers Crossed.

Fifth Attempt

We bussed it to San José one last time. We bypassed our lawyer's office and went directly to ScotiaBank by ourselves. We offered our paperwork and our banker offered us coffee.

After reviewing the paperwork the banker smiled and said, "congratulations." He created a total of four accounts – two for each of us, one of which is a "Dollars" account and the other is a "Colones" account. This will help with the management of two separate currencies.

After the accounts were set up, our broker wired the money we used to open the account with. Once the money was received, we moved it from the Dollars account to the Colones account and created a CD that will distribute interest every six months. The CD will earn, annualized, 6% - WOW.

We were elated, and left the bank not quite believing that we had opened an account, and were fully funded for our residency requirements.

54. No, they aren't cutting in line

So, I thought of a great business idea: kid rental. Yep, kid, as in child. You see, at many places in Costa Rica, the bank being one, if you have a young child, you get preferential treatment and you get to go to the front of the line regardless of what your bingo card says.

You will also get preferential treatment if you are old (hey, I could rent canes too!) and if you are pregnant (not sure how to capitalize on that one – pillow rental?).

It really is a great thing to witness the selfless act of someone being helped who is not in as good a situation as you. Many times you will see younger people give up their seats on a full bus so that an older person, pregnant person, or person with a young child, can sit. It is refreshing.

In the bank, however, it is actually mandated. There are signs that tell you as much and everyone pretty much complies without fuss.

55. ATMS

ATMs in Costa Rica are very much like the ATMs in North America. Once again, Costa Ricans like their security and many ATMs are behind a door that is locked. You can swipe your bankcard to unlock the door and once it is closed you are locked in and you have privacy. Usually, the outside window is clear or frosted so that you can see if someone is currently in the ATM area.

There are some things with ATMs here that you should be careful with:

- There recently was a scam involving ATMs in Costa Rica. Some of victims were in the town that I live in, Grecia. The scam is called skimming and it works like this: the bad guys install a card reader over the original card reader to capture your account information when you swipe your card. They also use a camera or a fake keypad to capture your PIN number. Once you swipe your card and type in your PIN they can access your account and have a good ole time – on you.

  To help protect yourself: if an ATM looks suspicious then don't use it, hide your actions with your free hand when you type in your PIN number, and review your bank account after each ATM use.

- Foreign ATM fees can be outrageous. In addition to the Costa Rican bank's fee for using a foreign card, your bank in the States may charge a foreign transaction fee, which is usually around 3%. Check with your bank and credit card to determine these fees before traveling.

- A friend of ours told us that once when she counted the money dispensed from her ATM transaction, she found that the ATM had dispensed too much money. Typical of most of our friends this one is honest and went into the bank to tell her story and return the errant bills.

The bank was thrilled.

Ever since hearing this story, I have counted the money given from each ATM transaction. The very first transaction I made after hearing our friend's story, of course, brought on a panic.

I am not often entrusted with functions regarding money (or laundry). So, when I am allowed to use the ATM I am a bit nervous to begin with.

Imagine my surprise when I requested 200,000 colones and a receipt but only got 80,000 colones with no receipt. To add to the confusion (and mounting fear) the ATM did not ask me its typical, "Do You Want Another Transaction" question. Instead it just rudely ejected my card, still without providing the requested receipt.

I admit, I was in a panic, less about the money and more about a potential failure. Luckily, I was at an ATM that had a full-service bank attached to it. I hit the red button to exit the locked room, took a few steps to the bank entrance, high fived the security guard, and told the teller my tale.

After calling a superior over we got to the bottom of the problem. The ATM was out of money, that was all. The additional money I had requested but was not paid-out was returned to my account. The teller gave me a receipt to prove it, and manually completed the balance of my transaction.

Moral of the story – don't count your chickens before they are hatched.

- One final tip regarding ATMs: once the machine ejects your card, GRAB IT! The ATMs in Costa Rica are notorious for ingesting the card back into the machine shortly after ejecting. This is a security measure and you can get your card back from the bank right away. Unless, of course it is after banking hours, on a weekend, or on one of the very many holidays.

CHAPTER 7 – Owning and driving a vehicle

Having a vehicle equals freedom. Here in Costa Rica it also equals a huge expense and potentially, huge headaches.

Vehicles have an import duty imposed on them that can only be described as "aggressive." The tax is weighted, based on the age of the vehicle, but any way you slice it the tax is oppressive. Here are the age ranges and the tax you will pay based on Costa Rica's valuation of your vehicle:

Current Model Year – 6 years old – 52%

7+years – 73%

The Ministerio de Hacienda website (www.hacienda.go.cr/autohacienda/autovalor.aspx) has a calculator to help you figure all the taxes involved with importing your car. The site is in Spanish, but you can use the Google Chrome browser to translate it.

In addition to the tax mentioned above, you still have to pay a shipper to deliver your vehicle to Costa Rica. This can add another $700 - $1,500, or more, depending on where you are shipping from.

The cost of freedom.

All of these costs are included when you purchase a vehicle here in Costa Rica. Add to that the fact that old vehicles retain their value here and you will find, even to buy a basic vehicle with 100,000 miles on it, you will be spending about 50% or more on it than you would in the U.S.

A good case could be made for just walking.

56. Driving, as a sport

Warning: driving in Costa Rica can cause chronic white knuckles.

Costa Ricans are relatively new to driving. The number of automobiles on the road has risen sharply over the past 10 years and more Ticos than ever are driving.

There are three main components that drive the danger:

First, when compared to the average driver in the U.S., the Tico driver has spent very little time behind the wheel. Think of half the cars on the Costa Rican roads as having a big sign in the rear window, "Driver in Training." Experience is key to avoiding accidents (and not causing accidents) and experience is one of the missing attributes of drivers throughout the country.

Secondly, add the cultural component of machismo to the mix; manly men driving aggressively without regard to other vehicles, road conditions, or speed. You will frequently see vehicles passing on a blind curve or passing when going up a hill, and they may pass on the left or the right depending on the mood.

We recently took the bus from San José to Guanacaste. It was a double decker bus and we had the interesting viewpoint of being on the second level near the front. The 5-hour trip was intense for us, having this bird's eye view. The highlight, in terms of crazy driving, was our bus driver deciding to pass an 18-wheeler laden with building materials. Granted the truck was only going about 20 kph (about 12 mph), but our driver decided to pass this truck whilst going up a hill. Needless to say we were about even with the truck, ready to overtake it, when a vehicle crested the hill, aimed right at us.

The battle ended in a stalemate with both our bus and the oncoming car stopped in the lane. Our bus driver moved back into the right side of the two-lane highway and fell back in behind the 18-wheeler, anxious to attempt to pass again. By the end of the trip my leg was sore from applying my phantom brake.

The third, and final, part of the white-knuckle experience is the condition of the roads. While Costa Rican roads have improved over the past few years it is still not uncommon to see a wood post or tree limb sticking up out of the road on what is considered a highway. This symbol of the Costa Rican driving experience simply means there is a pothole, a deep pothole, in the road and some thoughtful soul has pointed it out to other drivers.

It is not just potholes, the size of which could swallow a car, to worry about. Guardrails, or lack thereof, can be a problem. Costa Rica is a mountainous country and many roads go up and down these mountains – with steep, sometimes sheer, drop offs and no guardrails.

The moral of the story is that to drive in Cost Rica you must drive both aggressively and defensively. Also it helps to have a cold Imperial waiting for you at your destination – make it a michelada.

57. Look both ways. Wait. Now run!

Since we are discussing the aggressiveness and lack of experience of Costa Rican drivers, let's talk about the flip-side of the driving coin – what to expect when you are a pedestrian.

Whether by law or de jure, pedestrians do not have the right-of-way in Costa Rica and, because stoplights and stop signs are merely suggestions, it is very important to be a defensive walker.

If you are about to walk in front of a stopped car it is a great idea to make eye contact and motion with your hand that you would like to cross in front of him without being run over. Normally, they will smile and wave you on, but if you do not get the go ahead, do not go ahead. Just wait it out, because he probably is in a hurry, or did not see you, or he is exercising his right of way rights.

One additional tip for walking: If you think you will be smart and walk behind a vehicle stopped at a stop sign – an oxymoron, I know - be sure to give plenty of space. Once again, we are talking about a very hilly country and the majority of vehicles have standard transmissions (that means stick-shift) and will roll backward slightly (or greatly), before going forward, when they are at rest on a hill.

58. Buckle up – it's the law

Many older vehicles, especially utilitarian SUVs like the old Land Cruisers and Land Rovers, do not have seatbelts for the rear seats. In Costa Rica all available seats must have a functioning seatbelt whether or not a passenger ever uses that seat.

And just like in the U.S. you must buckle up in Costa Rica. However, unlike in the States, rear passengers must buckle up as well.

59. Crash/help kit

Every vehicle must have the following items in the vehicle in case of accident or emergency: fire extinguisher, lug wrench, jack, reflective vests, first aid kit, and a reflective triangle.

Fines in Costa Rica can be very steep so it is best to be in compliance with the law. And for the law requiring this kit and the law above regarding seatbelts, they make a lot of sense.

60. What to do in a wreck

If you are in a wreck in Costa Rica, it is important that you do a couple of things that are a bit different than in the States.

First, recognize that you are a Gringo and are at an automatic disadvantage – especially if you don't speak Spanish (you do know you are in Central America, right? - where Spanish is the language?).

If both parties agree that there is no damage, or agree to a settlement, then the work is done and you can go on your merry way. I would imagine if this is the case, a couple of witnesses, some pictures from your cell-phone, or video, might come in handy down the road.

If, on the other hand, there is damage and/or injuries, there will be bureaucracy and you must go through a process:

- DO NOT MOVE YOUR VEHICLE. Even if you are blocking a major intersection during rush hour. It does not matter that people are honking and yelling at you. Do not move your vehicle until a traffic cop arrives.

- If there are injuries, dial 911. Although not possessing anywhere near the sophistication and response time of the U.S. 911 system, Costa Rica does have a 911 service, centralized in San José, where they will try to coordinate with the appropriate facilities in the area nearest your accident.

- Now is a good time to grab that reflective triangle from your kit and place it about 15 feet from the back of your vehicle.

- Call the transit police (2222-9330 or 2222-9245) and INS (800-800-8000). The transit police are needed to write the initial ticket that will start the process of resolution. INS is the Costa Rican government entity that handles the *marchamo* – mandatory liability auto insurance.

- Write down information: license plate number, description of accident, witness names and contact information, etc.

- After the initial ticket is written, review it and call a tow truck if necessary. Be sure to have your vehicle towed to a garage that is authorized by INS or you will have to have it towed again.

- Go to court to file a report of the accident (you have 10 days to do this). Ask the transit police the location of the court, as it will most likely be the courthouse closest to the scene of the accident.

- When you file the report at the courthouse a court date will be set for a hearing to determine who was at fault.

- Do not allow work to begin on your vehicle before this report has been made at the courthouse. If you do, insurance might not cover the expense.

Sometimes I love not having a vehicle.

61. Riteve

Riteve (www.rtv.co.cr) is the annual inspection of older cars or biannual (I use biannual here to mean every two years not twice a year – the word can be defined both ways – English can be a crazy language) inspection of newer cars. Items that are checked are tires, emissions, lights (brake and headlights), as well as other items.

The inspection is rigorous and it is not unusual for a vehicle to fail. A re-inspection costs less than the initial inspection.

There are clever ways, I have heard, to pass the inspection. There is actually a cottage industry built around the riteve. Remember how I was joking about renting children and canes outside the bank? Well, this is no joke – there are places where you can rent a set of tires, a brake light, or any other item that is deficient on your vehicle that might cause you to fail the inspection, so that you can now pass.

I have heard that some geniuses (probably Gringos) have tried taping a $20 somewhere in the engine compartment as a bribe to let a sub-par vehicle pass; finders keepers, right? Well, losers weepers because the vehicle still failed inspection, but the mechanic was happy with his newfound cash.

By far the strategy used most by Gringos is to take the vehicle to their personal mechanic for a pre-inspection inspection. Then have the mechanic take it to the official inspection site to handle the certification and any questions. To handle the inspection oneself requires excellent Spanish, specifically technical terms relating to vehicles.

The month riteve is due is based on the last digit of the vehicle's license plate. Upon successfully completing the inspection, a sticker is issued and is placed on the passenger's side of the windshield.

It is important to be up-to-date on riteve. Transit police will often have stop points set up just to look for out-of-date stickers. Fines for not having a current riteve are a great boon to the local economy. You don't have to contribute in this way, you know?

62. License plate numerology

As mentioned above, there is significance to the last digit of the Costa Rican license plate. In addition to providing a clue regarding the month riteve is due, the last digit also indicates the day of the week on which you are prohibited to drive your vehicle in San José.

This restriction is designed to reduce traffic and congestion in the capital city and it is in effect from 6am – 7pm on the day the license plate denotes. It works like this: if the last digit of your license plate ends in the number one or two then you are restricted on Mondays. If your plate ends in number three or four, then your restricted day is Tuesday, and so on through zero and Friday.

Buses, taxis, tourist vans, and motorcycles are not restricted and can drive any day and any time in the capital city regardless of the last number on their license plates.

63. Gas stations

You can't judge a book by its cover. While gas stations in Costa Rica look exactly like those found in the States, they operate very differently.

To begin with, gas prices are regulated by the government, so there is zero competition and what you pay at one station will be the exact same price you pay at any other gas station in the country.

Also, in Costa Rica, you will never pump your own gas, even if you want to. Full service is the only option. Just like in the olden days in the States, in addition to pumping your gas, the attendant may wash your windshield, top off water levels, and check your tire pressure. Just let them know what you would like them to do.

Tipping a couple hundred colones is customary if the attendant does anything more than pump the gas.

64. Protecting your investment

Vehicle theft can be a problem in Costa Rica, just like anywhere else. It is important to make things difficult for would-be thieves, as most examples of theft are crimes of opportunity.

The first tip is: don't be an idiot. Never, ever, ever, leave valuables in a vehicle – whether it is locked or unlocked. Smash and grab type theft is probably the most common form of theft and the most easily avoided.

If you are stopping at a restaurant, store, or tourist stop, try to park your vehicle so that it can remain in your sight.

Many people purchase products that can safeguard their vehicle from theft. Lug-locks are great to protect your wheels and tires, not because the thief can't get the special lug off, but because it adds to the amount of time and hassle it takes to remove the wheel.

Another visible deterrent is the famous Club, a long bar that locks on to the steering wheel causing the vehicle to be undrivable even if it was hotwired. Again, the Club is not a failsafe method, but it does take the convenience factor away from the thieves.

Finally, there are the unseen installed items that can help keep your car your car. A kill switch can be installed in a hidden place and when toggled off the car will not start, even if hotwired. The switch works by cutting off the flow of electricity from the battery and keeps people from hotwiring the vehicle. Then there is always the dreaded car alarm that everyone hates and that alarms no one at all.

65. License to drive

Back in the good ole days, about two years ago, one could go to the Costa Rican equivalent of the DMV (called COSEVI) take a test, have a "medical evaluation" and be issued a Costa Rica Driver's License.

No más.

Now, in order to get a license, you must be a resident, i.e., you must possess a Cedula. The good news is that your U.S. driver's license is valid for use in Costa Rica for as long as your tourist visa allows you to be in country.

The bad news, for those in residential limbo like me, is that Immigration and COSEVI operate independently of each other. Because my residency is "in progress" and I have been issued an *expediente* (expediency) number and am no longer required to leave the country every 90 days to renew my tourist visa.

However, if I were to drive (which I don't), I would still have to leave the country every 90 days just so my Texas drivers license would remain valid.

Once my residency application is completed, and I am issued a Cedula, I could get a Costa Rican license. Once this is issued I would not have to leave the country every 90 days to keep my Texas license valid in Costa Rica.

66. Driving takes its toll (sometimes)

There are toll roads in Costa Rica. They operate in much the same way as they do in the U.S. There are three exceptions:

First, there is no automatic "EZ Pay" type of system for those who do not have a bank account. You, Gringo, must pay the requisite amount in coins or cash, unless of course you are able to open a bank account, which means, establishing residency, owning property, or a Costa Rican corporation.

The second way the toll roads are different from ones in the States is that when traffic is too heavy on a Costa Rican toll road they just stop taking tolls and open up each lane to clear the congestion. Function over finance – I love it.

Finally, on major holidays, a few lucky toll payers will receive a gift bag filled with household items and goodies donated by various local businesses. These are usually given out at Christmas time and only a limited number are given out. Once they are gone, they're gone.

67. Where the streets have no names

First time visitors to Costa Rica are often times bewildered with the address and street sign system in the country - mainly because there is no system for such things.

The reality is that the streets *do* have names, just not consistent signage with most areas not having any signs at all. Downtown San José is the exception – the major streets there are well marked.

House numbers are also lacking through out the country, and addresses are more of a description of how to get (close) to a home or business. Occasionally an official address (description) will have a reference point that no longer exists, like a large tree or other landmark that has been moved or destroyed.

Most addresses basically provide points of references as well as a street description so that you can get close. They look something like:

"On the el Cajón ridge the home is 100 meters North of the Los Angeles church, left side of street, two story green house."

You can't miss it!

As you spend time in the country, you learn to get around and you will find that it is not as challenging as you would think. Navigation devices can be loaded with Costa Rican maps (if you are renting a vehicle you can rent navigation as well). These maps are relatively complete and can help you get (close) to your destination.

There is also a free app for smart phones that is a must have. Waze is a community-based app and is an incredible pocket navigation resource that will cost you nothing. Also, it pings off of satellites and does not use your phone minutes.

Here are some directional Spanish terms to help when you (this is primarily for the ladies, 'cause we know the men won't) have to ask for directions.

As, this book is not a Spanish book I am giving you "caveman" Spanish so you can grunt your way to your destination – no complete sentences here.

inside – adentro
outside – afuera (great to know for al fresco dining)
to the left – a la izquierda
to the right – a la derecha
here – aquí
near – cerca
far – lejos
where is? – ¿dónde ésta?
up – arriba (you just thought of Speedy Gonzales, right?)
down – abajo
street – calle
avenue - avenida
North – Norte
South – Sur
East – Este
West - Oeste

68. Honky-tonk

When you are driving in the U.S. and someone honks his or her car horn at you, you can be sure that what the driver is trying to convey involves an expletive.

"Get out of my f'n way."
"You f'n moron."
"Where did you f'n learn to drive?"

It is almost like the viciousness you see on forums and social media except that people are hiding behind a steering wheel instead of a keyboard.

In Costa Rica things are a bit different. Vehicles honk frequently, incessantly, but rarely as a result of road rage or driver emotional imbalance.

More likely the meaning is something like:

"I am passing you now, just wanted to let you know."
"Hey Juan, good to see you."
"Hey baby, you are looking GOOOOD."
"Thanks."
"Dude, you are about to back up into a ditch."

Very rarely have I seen the horn in Costa Rica used the way it is in the States, as a blunt instrument. It is one of the few good things about driving here.

69. Wachimen

As you are driving around a town, if you are not going home or to a friend's house, you will need to park somewhere. Luckily for you Costa Rica has a system for that.

In most towns, where there is street parking (and sometimes in parking lots) there will be a wachiman. I am not sure if the wachimen are self-appointed or if the town appoints them. I do know that they take their role of showing you where to park, guiding you in and out of tight parking spaces, and collecting a couple of hundred colones, very seriously.

Another type of parking system can be seen at public buildings, like the shopping mall and airport. This system is a ticketing system, and the way it is normally implemented causes much confusion.

As you enter the parking area you will be given a ticket (either by a person or a machine). The trouble comes when it is time to leave. Instead of paying at the exit gate, as one would expect, you must walk to a centralized kiosk (typically far from the exit gate and only accessible on foot) to pay and get your receipt. You will need this receipt to put in the machine at the exit so that the mechanical arm will lift and let you out of the parking area.

If the problem with this system is not obvious to you I will point it out. If you are new to the country and new to this type of parking system, it is not likely that you will think about the necessity of paying for your parking before you exit. So what happens is cars at the exit get backed up because someone at the front did not get their ticket and they can't exit.

Everyone behind the offender has to now back up so he can get out of line to get his ticket, or wait while the driver sends a passenger to go fetch the ticket. I see it happen every time I go to the airport and every time I go to a certain mall. Now you know.

CHAPTER 8 – The bus

Living in Dallas, Texas, we never used public transportation, despite the efficiencies and cost savings of the DART (Dallas Area Rapid Transit) system.

Instead, Jen and I would pull out of our home garage each morning, each in our own cars, and commute to our respective offices that were no more than a mile from each other and only 7 miles from our home from garage to garage. An even sadder fact is that directly outside my office was a light-rail terminal that could have delivered me to and from work for about $2 a day.

For us, when we lived in the States, life was about convenience. We were what some called DINKS – Dual Income No Kids – and we could afford two cars; afford ease, afford waste.

When we decided to simplify our lives and move to this Central American country, we decided that we would live without the expense of a car, at least initially – to see how it would go.

Public transportation is the standard method of getting from point A to point B for the majority of the Costa Rican populace. Busses are reliable, affordable, and can take you to many places in the country as well as outside the country, and not only to the border countries of Nicaragua and Panama, but to El Salvador, Honduras, Guatemala and more.

Beginning with our first tentative trip into town when we first arrived in our new home, a bus ride where we did not know when to pull the cord to tell the driver where to stop – hell, we didn't even know there WAS a cord to pull – we have learned a lot about riding the bus.

Now it is fun to just take off and explore, venturing further and further from our comfort zone. And although it is still a bit stressful heading out to places unknown, it is a wonderful(ly cheap) way to travel.

Below are some tips and observations that we have learned that can help you get accustomed to travel by bus faster. It really is a great way to see the country, especially for those on a budget.

70. When in Costa Rica

The sun in Costa Rica can be brutal and when you are pinned to your bus seat unable to move away from the intense sunlight streaming in through the window, you will thank me for this tip.

When you first get on a bus, if you see one side filling up while the other side is relatively empty, join the crowd. Everyone on the bus (but you) knows where the sun will be along the route and they are sitting on the best side to avoid it.

71. Pick a station (not just) any station

There are over 15 different bus stations in the capital city of San José and these stations are spread, far and wide, throughout the city. You need to choose the right one in order to get on the correct bus for your destination.

When we are in San José, and are ready to return home, we have a taxi take us to the Grecia Station. This station serves Grecia, Sarchí and Naranjo in the Central Valley. The bus ride from this station to Grecia takes about an hour and costs about $2 per person each way and leaves, during rush hour, every 20 to 30 minutes. Each station and route has its own pricing structure and schedule.

We recently took a trip to the beach in Guanacaste, a province in the northwest part of the country on the Pacific coast. For this trip we took the bus from Grecia to San José, then took a cab to the Pulmitan de Liberia station, which services Playas del Coco and Liberia. We had to be careful and clear to let the cab know it was the Liberia station as there are two Pulmitan bus stations.

This bus cost $8 per person each way, and delivered us 5 hours away to the beach town of Playas del Coco. The ride included a 30 minute pit-stop half way through for snacks and a restroom. The bus did not have an on board bathroom, but it was air-conditioned and, surprisingly, the seats fit my 6'4" frame well.

72. Gonna hitch a ride

The first time someone told me I could catch a bus on the side of the highway I figured they were pulling my leg.

They weren't. Many bus stops are on the side of the road. Let me rephrase that, you can catch many buses on the side of the road – whether or not there is a bus stop. Not just any road, mind you: highways, freeways, and the expressway. There is no extra lane for the bus to stop; it just stops in the outermost lane, other traffic be damned.

The hard part about the freeway bus stop (other than the fear factor) is being able to read the name of your bus as it is barreling down the road toward you at 80 kph (that would be… oh, go figure it out yourself).

If you do not recognize your bus in time to wave it down, it will just pass you by. One time, I flagged down a bus that was not going to our destination to ask the driver a question. I asked the question, he answered, and I resumed my flag-down stance on the side of the road.

The driver drove away, not amused.

73. Home delivery?

For the price of bus fare you can have a package delivered to any stop along the bus's route. In small communities, like the one I live in, this means home delivery. Someone in town hands the driver a package and the correct amount of change, and he will deliver it to the appropriate house.

This is also useful for items you may need from San José. Being the capital city and the largest city in the country, San José has the largest variety of items, including hard-to-get, imported items. Many times a pharmacy prescription can only be filled in San José. There is no need for you to make a trip though; the pharmacist will make sure it gets on the bus and you can pick it up at the agreed upon bus stop.

This delivery service is not just for small items. All buses have storage compartments on the outside for luggage and other cargo. I have seen a 25 Kilogram bag of potatoes (that is 55 lbs for you guys in the U.S. – are you with me yet?) to someone's front door. What a great service.

74. Bond, James Bond

No, the bus drivers do not drink a martini (shaken or stirred) while they are driving. What I mean to say is that they are very competent drivers. And they have to be since the roads and drivers in Costa Rica, as we have discussed, are not for the faint of heart. Many roads are pothole laden and some are only wide enough to fit one and a half cars, not to mention a bus and a car, or two buses passing in the night.

I have seen these drivers pass within an inch of another vehicle and maneuver past obstacles where I was certain something was going to be crushed. Instead, the driver calculates, slowly makes his move, and continues on. It truly is incredible to watch.

75. Drive thru Costa Rica

Traffic jams create opportunities for local vendors to make a sale. Often times, when traffic is stacked up at a toll booth or because of road construction, there will be Ticos selling fruits, plantain chips, natural juices or other typical Costa Rican snacks to those waiting in traffic, even those on the bus.

On longer bus trips, the driver will often allow one of these sellers on the bus to sell to the passengers. The sales person will get on at one bus stop and get off at the next and in between walk through the bus cabin offering goodies for purchase. After walking through he will pay the driver his bus fare from the proceeds before he gets off – the price of doing business.

One of the items sold by these vendors is fruit juice and the packaging might surprise you. Basically, the juice is placed in a clear plastic bag, like a sandwich bag, instead of a plastic bottle. You bite off the end of the plastic bag, or use the straw they give you, and suck down the fruity goodness -- different, but refreshing.

76. El autobús musical chairs

One of the fascinating things to watch on the bus is what I call musical chairs. I have mentioned the elevated status of elderly people and those who are pregnant or traveling with young children. There is no better place to witness this than when you are riding on the bus.

As the bus fills up, you will see young and able bodied passengers give up their seats to allow older passengers and pregnant women to sit. This is especially true for the seats toward the front of the bus that are closer to the doors. It is refreshing to see people offer their assistance.

77. Time for change

The bus driver can make change for just about any denomination of Costa Rican currency. For change back on larger bills, many times the driver must wait until the bus fills in order to provide change back. It is interesting to watch as he keeps track of how much he owes each person.

78. Get in the back

In Costa Rica many people use the bus system; in fact more residents use public transportation than those that don't. Because of this, the buses fill up. Completely. Not only are all the seats taken but there will also be multiple people standing in the aisles.

Occasionally when this happens, the standing area in the front is filled up but there is room in the back. So the driver will ask you to get on the bus through the back door.

On each bus is an electrical passenger counter. It is usually two parallel black posts on either side of the entry steps. The important thing to know is that when the driver asks you to get on in the back you should not pass the counter in the front, as there is one in the back as well.

The first time this happened to me I was trying to juggle grocery bags, and rapid fire Spanish being thrown at me and I passed through the counter just in time to figure out what I was being told, that I needed to get on through the back door. Realizing my mistake, I immediately backed through the counter again. I looked at the driver who had a scowl on his face and then I realized I had change in my hand and had to pay.

Of course I stepped forward to pay (and be counted again.) And for good measure, I passed back through the counter one last time as I tumbled down the steps and made my way to the back door of the bus, my head hung in shame.

79. Theft and scams

Even though the bus is a great mode of transportation and can be safe, precautions need to be taken to keep your belongings yours; this is especially true on the buses that service the larger cities or those that are traveling long distances.

It is a good idea to ignore the overhead compartments designed to store your stuff, and instead keep your belongings on your lap or between your legs.

One common method thieves use to separate you from your possessions is to work in unison with a partner. When the bus stops and everyone is exiting the bus, one of the thieves (who maneuvered to be in front of you) drops something, or falls, or does some other dramatic thing to elicit your desire to assist. As you help the poor soul, his partner helps himself to your stuff.

The best way to avoid this scam is to sit at the very front of the bus and be the first one off or to wait until everyone disembarks before leaving your seat.

If you do find yourself in the situation I described above, grab your purse or backpack and put your hand over your wallet because someone is about to try and grab them.

Pickpockets and grab and dash are the other ways thieves will steal from you on the bus. Pickpockets will "accidently" bump into you and while they are in close quarters, help themselves to what ever is loose in your pockets.

The grab and dash guys do just that – they see something that is loose (a purse or backpack), grab it and run away, expecting that you will be too stunned to give chase right away.

To avoid having to run after someone, don't use the overhead storage bins on the bus, and wear your purse strap across your chest as opposed to just over your arm. When seated, I like to use one of the clip-able straps on my backpack and clip it somewhere to me; if the backpack is between my legs, I will clip the strap around my leg or if the backpack is on my lap, I will clip the strap to a belt buckle. Overkill? Maybe, but I have never had my backpack stolen, and I know some friends who have.

CHAPTER 9 – The animals

Costa Rica is one of the most bio-diverse places on Earth. It therefore may not surprise you that there are a lot of different animals here.

Whole books have been written about individual species and my little book is only briefly touching on some of the interesting things I have seen.

80. The most common animal

You cannot go very far in Costa Rica without encountering a dog. He will be outside, chained or loose. He may be well fed or his ribs may be the most prominent aspect of his body.

Dogs in Costa Rica are considered protection, pets, pests, and problems. Many are community mutts (Zaguates) fed and cared for by the neighborhood at large.

Some guard unfenced yards, snapping at the heels of walkers-by. Some are friendly, and some are fierce. And then there are the strays, the feral, desperately roaming the streets, digging through trash looking for a scrap of nutrition. It is estimated that there are over one million stray dogs in Costa Rica.

Dogs in Costa Rica, even the pets, are not treated the same way as most dogs in North America. It can be heart breaking to see all the help that is needed for dogs here. Because dogs are treated more like property than as a member of the family, they are often malnourished and do not receive the veterinary care that they need. Most are not spayed or neutered and because they are not kept in an enclosed area they have puppies – lots of puppies, perpetuating the problem.

Not a happy problem in the happiest country in the world, but one that visitors should be aware of.

81. Cock-a-doodle-do

The male chicken, also known as a rooster, or a cock, is a venerated animal in Costa Rica. OK, maybe not venerated, but its colorful plumage imagery has been used to describe colorful Costa Rican food items such as:

Gallo Pinto – a typical Costa Rican meal of rice and beans mixed with vegetables.

and

Pico de Gallo – a colorful array of diced tomato, onion and cilantro.

If you haven't figured it out, *gallo* in Spanish is rooster. So he is indeed venerated, verbally venerated.

One interesting thing about the rooster is that he is not essential for a hen to produce eggs. He is only needed for the eggs to be fertilized so they can hatch into chicks. If you just want eggs to eat, no rooster is needed.

Someone should tell this to my neighbor.

82. Monkeying around

Costa Rica is home to 4 different species of monkey:

White Headed Capuchin
Ranges from Honduras to Ecuador. The white headed capuchin is often seen begging in beach areas where they have become accustomed to being fed. DO NOT feed the monkeys, even bananas. It is not healthy for them.

The capuchin monkey is one of the most recognizable monkeys thanks to its work in film and TV. The monkey on NBC's hit sitcom *Friends*, named Marcel, was a capuchin, as was the star who brought the virus to the masses in *Outbreak* and the monkey that liked gold in *Pirates of the Caribbean*.

Geoffroy's Spider Monkey
The spider monkey ranges from Mexico through Panama and is considered endangered by the IUCN (The International Union for the Conservation of Nature, the world's main authority on conservation of species) mainly due to habitat loss.

It is one of the largest of the New World Monkeys, weighing in at 20 pounds and is rarely seen in the film industry.

Central American Squirrel Monkey (the Ticos call it a Titi)

Range is the southern portion of Costa Rica and Panama. It is, in my humble opinion, the cutest of the four monkey species found here – I figured you would want to know that.

The squirrel monkey is the smallest and lightest of the four monkey species, the male being larger than the female and weighing in as a featherweight at just under two pounds.

Like the spider monkey, the squirrel monkey is rarely seen in films.

Mantled Howler Monkey (the Ticos call it a Congo monkey)

The howler monkey's range is the same as the white headed capuchin's: Honduras to Ecuador. Also, like the capuchin, the howler is a common sight and sound in Costa Rica and he is not endangered.

Unlike the capuchin, the howler's work in movies has been relegated to voice-over work thanks to its haunting howl. Surprisingly, it was the howler monkey that provided the cries of some of the dinosaurs in *Jurassic Park*.

Most of the monkey species are readily seen in tourist areas. The exception is the Spider Monkey, because it is endangered and because of its range. The only place you can see all four monkey species in one place is Corcovado National Park on the Osa Peninsula.

83. Not just a deadly sin

The sloth is a fascinating animal to see in the wild. They move extremely slowly, so slowly that algae can form on them. Beetles, moths and mites use the sloth as a place to live, and will leave the sloth to deposit their eggs in the sloth's dung.

The sloth has a very slow digestive process and only leaves the protection of the trees once a week to travel to the forest floor to defecate. Its diet consists entirely of different varieties of leaves; the animal will move from tree to tree so that he receives the range of nutrients he needs from eating different foliage.

There are two varieties of sloth in Costa Rica.

- Hoffman's Two Toed Sloth
- Three Toed Sloth

The life span for a sloth in the wild is nearly three times that of one in captivity. Luckily, aside from rescue organizations, only a few are held in captivity and those illegally.

84. Scarlet fever

Tied with the monkey and sloth as the most "must see" animals that visitors to Costa Rica want to view is the Scarlet Macaw.

Measuring in at 32 inches (I mean 81 centimeters), the macaw is not a small bird. Its size, along with bright colors of blue, red, and yellow, makes it difficult to miss.

Finding one can be a challenge though. Because of habitat destruction and illegal pet trade, the macaw's range in Costa Rica has dwindled to two main areas on the Pacific coast: the Carara National Park and the Osa Peninsula.

The macaw can be seen in other places (we saw a pair near the infamous Tárcoles River Bridge recently) but the aforementioned areas give you the best bet of spotting them.

Macaws mate for life and are almost always seen in pairs. Their diet consists mainly of fruits, nuts, and seeds – almonds being their favorite; it is the tree they are most likely to be found in.

85. An unlikely celebrity

When choosing its national bird, one might think that Costa Rica would have chosen the macaw both for its size and beauty, or the interesting and colorful toucan, or one of the many other brightly clothed birds flying around the country.

Instead, in 1977, the country designated the clay-colored thrush (originally named the clay-colored robin) as its national bird. There is no greater indication that Costa Rica is dependent on farming than the choice of this unassuming bird as its national symbol. The clay-colored thrush, in Spanish *yigüirro*, mates between April and June, with the male of the species belting a melodic tune to woo a mate. The breeding season coincides with the start of rainy season thus the song of the thrush is a positive omen for the farmers.

86. Venomous snakes

There are at least 20 species of venomous snakes in Costa Rica. I have bestowed the following honorary titles to my favorite venomous serpents that live here.

The Most Feared - Arguably, the most feared venomous snake is the fer-de-lance, called *terciopelo* in Spanish or "velvet" because of its velvet-like skin; most feared because of its aggressiveness.

Many snakes, when confronted with a danger will flee, saving valuable venom resources. Not the fer-de-lance; it produces copious amounts of venom and this is one reason, it is thought, that it will defend its territory and move toward a threat instead of away.

The Most Deadly - The most deadly of venomous snakes in Costa Rica is the rarely seen bush master.

There are three species of bush masters in existence, two of which reside in Costa Rica. The snake is large and can reach lengths to ten feet, though six to eight feet is more common.

Luckily for all of us, the bush master is rarely encountered. He is a secretive sort and does not have the aggressive nature of the fer-de-lance, although I wouldn't go petting one.

The Most Colorful - I have to call this category a tie. And I choose the coral snake of "red touch yellow, kill a fellow" fame and the gold-colored eyelash pit viper.

A neighbor of mine was bitten by a coral snake. He stepped on it and the snake did not really like that, so he bit into the man's bare toe. Luckily this was in Grecia, home to the not-so-famous World of Snakes, and anti-venom was readily available at the hospital and no long-term health issues ensued because of this mishap.

87. Other creepy crawlies

When Jen and I were looking at Costa Rica as a place to retire, one of the considerations were bugs. My wife hates them, and while Texas had its share we lived in a very populated area, minimizing many of the bigger critters. Those that were left we handled with quarterly extermination treatments.

Now that we have lived in Costa Rica for a while I can tell you that bugs are ever-present here, but you can still live in harmony. Mostly, they stay outside and many people spray a poison inside to ensure that any bug on the inside will die.

We live at an elevation of 1430 meters (that is _____ feet?) and the coolness at our elevation gives us a different bug parade than one might expect at the beach. Still, there is a small basket of bugs that are most feared.

Tarantulas – horror films love to feature these large, eight-legged creeps and they are prevalent throughout Costa Rica. Typically, much smaller than the giants on the big screen (even those not affected by radioactivity), tarantulas within the country are nocturnal and do not spin webs but rather live in a burrow in the ground. They are awesome at killing and eating the other pests that you hate seeing.

Roaches – those nasty things, they live here too. Luckily, poison and spiders can help keep them at bay. I have not encountered here the giant "water bug" type that is frequently seen in Texas.

Cata-killers – ok, so maybe not "killers" per se, but some of Costa Rica's caterpillars can pack a punch, leaving the person who touched it with an awful rash. Even though they are colorful and cute in their furriness, please don't pet the caterpillars.

Scorpions – these suckers (stingers) freak even me out, and I like bugs, spiders, and snakes. It is not that their sting is so painful, it is not – one stung me on my third day here. It's just that they are so menacing looking. Like the tarantula, the scorpion can be found in clothes and shoes everywhere throughout the country. Unlike the tarantula the scorpion glows in the dark when it is exposed to a black light.

CHAPTER 10 – Staying connected

For those visiting or moving to Costa Rica, there is nothing quite as important as being able to post to Facebook a picture of the food you are eating to let your friends know that you are eating in a foreign country.

Luckily for everyone Costa Rica is, mostly, wired. There is Internet access that runs the gamut from poor to excellent, cell phone service available throughout the country via several different companies, and there are free and paid services to help you stay connected to home.

While the services might not be up to North American standards, and they might go out more frequently, and they might take longer to fix, they exist here and they make life easier. This wired'ness allows visitors to stay connected to friends and family, both at home and within the country. From cell phones to free video chat, visiting and living in a wired country makes using technology to stay connected easier.

88. Wi-Fi hot spots

Cell phones, tablets, and laptops are all important pieces of technology that can help with navigation, finding information on places to visit, bus schedules, or any number of other things throughout the country.

Costa Rica is becoming very wired. I guess it is really unwired, with many Wi-Fi hotspots throughout each town. Most public places such as bus terminals, central parks, and malls have non-password protected signals, while access available at restaurants and other locations will most likely require a password.

89. Living in a cell

One of the great aspects of quitting my job, selling everything, and moving to Costa Rica, has been the ability to disconnect from technology and start connecting with people.

The cellphone in my previous life was permanently attached either to my hip, ear, or at a minimum, within earshot on my nightstand while I slept. Now, it is nothing for me to leave the house for an entire day without having my phone with me. However, if I do have the phone with me and it rings, I must answer it.

Baby steps.

Most visitors to Costa Rica will want to be able to have a cell phone to make calls within the country, to communicate with hotels, restaurants, and of course, to get directions. Luckily, this is easy enough to do.

I am not going to discuss using your U.S. phone plan here as there are just too many variables to properly address the subject. Instead, we will discuss buying a SIM card that will give you a pay-as-you-go Costa Rican cell phone number.

You can purchase a SIM card from kiosks at both international airports when you fly in, assuming of course your flight arrives during normal business hours.

There are also phone stores in most malls, in even the smallest town, and at each of the borders of the country. Basically, anywhere there are people there are SIM cards available.

There are four main companies from which you can buy service: Movistar, Claro, Kolbi, and Tu Yo Móval. If you are traveling throughout the country, Kolbi, which is the oldest service, has the best overall coverage.

Otherwise, each company has its locational strengths. For example, where I live, eight miles up in the mountains outside of Grecia, Kolbi doesn't work as well as Movistar so we have Movistar.

It is now possible to switch carriers and keep your same phone number. So, if one company does not work well for your area you can just change carriers – no harm, no foul. This was not the case a year ago.

In order to get cell service in Costa Rica (with a Costa Rican phone number) you must have an unlocked cell phone and it must be a Quad Band or GSM phone. If your U.S. cell phone cannot be unlocked or is not a GSM phone your best bet is to buy a "burner," i.e. a throw away phone. You can pick up a very basic phone here for under $50.

After those requirements are met, you just need to purchase a pay-as-you-go-plan from a vendor as only permanent residents are able to have a contract. You will pay between $4 and $6 for the SIM card and initial load of minutes, and you will need to have your passport in order to activate service.

It is wise to have the vendor install the SIM card while you are there. This way they can clip it if it is the wrong size, and program and test the phone for you before you leave. Trust me on this. My iPhone 4s takes the micro sized SIM and all plans here come with the standard sized SIM.

I bought my plan from a guy on the roadside: it was a great deal. For $4 I got the card/phone number and $6 worth of minutes. The only problem was that it was the wrong sized card. I had to make an additional trip downtown and pay a store $2 to cut the card to fit. With the latest model phones, using even smaller "nano" sized cards, you will most likely need to get it cut.

You can fill up your phone at just about any store, at a mall, at bus stations, just about everywhere. To fill it up you just give your number to the clerk, state the name of the phone company and how much you want to load.

Rates are set by the government and do not fluctuate from company to company. The loaded minutes can be used for phone calls or as data. A call anywhere within Costa Rica is considered a local call.

Here are some emergency and helpful numbers to program into your phone for your visit here:

911 – All Emergencies
117 – Police
118 – Fire

90. Seeing is believing

Since retiring to Costa Rica I spend more time talking with friends and family back home than I did when we lived in the same city. Technology makes speaking with and seeing your loved ones easy.

Oh, and it is free too.

There are three main programs that can be used for video calls, all three free.

My wife and I are an Apple family and we have all the iProducts so we use FaceTime for our video chatting needs. The only drawback to FaceTime is that it is only designed for Apple products, so both participants must be using one of the iProducts.

Skype is another free video/call program. It can be a beast to set up an account. But once you've done it, you can communicate easily with anyone else who has a Skype account.

The new kid on the block is Facebook video messaging. In the private messaging screen on the social media giant's page, there is now an icon for video chat. Click it and set up your account and you are ready to go.

All three of these technologies allow you stay connected to home, wherever that may be, and see the people you are talking to. It goes without saying (I hope) that you need an Internet connection and a device with both a microphone and web camera in order to use these services.

91. Communicating old school - kinda

Phone calls are still a very important form of communication. Luckily, there are low cost alternatives to long distance/overseas calling. Using Wi-Fi networks, services like Viber and MagicJack offer quality communication; one for free, one for cheap.

Viber is relatively new but is an incredible resource. The app facilitates free phone calls and texting from anywhere in the world via a Wi-Fi signal to anyone who also has the Viber app.

MagicJack has been around the longest of any of the VOIP services and it is a service that we use frequently. There are two ways to use the service. First there is a USB apparatus that you attach to your computer and then plug in a corded phone – our experience with this method has led us to not use this method.

You can also download the app for your cell phone. This method works very well as long as you have a good Wi-Fi signal.

MagicJack does cost money; we paid $50 for the crappy USB apparatus (this is mandatory) and then $120 for 5 years worth of service. The great thing about MagicJack is that you are assigned a phone number from whatever city you wish (within the U.S. and Canada). So, even though we no longer have U.S. based cell phone plans, we still have a Dallas phone number (thorough MJ).

Costa Rica does have landline service. It is difficult for a non-resident to get one though. Because of this, many times, the landline is passed on to the new owner of a home or a renter.

Most phone numbers in Costa Rica are eight digits. Like many things here there are anomalies; for the phone companies the phone numbers are only four digits long.

To dial Costa Rica when you are outside the country you need the following components: exit code (011), country code (506), and then phone number (xxxx-xxxx). Put it all together and a Costa Rican phone number, dialed from North America, looks like this 011-506-xxxx-xxxx. Inside the country you can drop the exit code and country code and just use the eight digit number.

92. Hide and seek

One of the tools you may want to invest in if you move to Costa Rica (or any other country) is a VPN (Virtual Private Network) service. A VPN secures your Internet connection allowing you to maintain privacy when sending or receiving data. There are many reasons people would want to use a VPN, two of which are particularly useful to the expat.

First, the VPN allows you to avoid geographic restrictions when accessing certain websites and content.

For example, Netflix has different programing for their services if you are in Costa Rica or in the U.S. A VPN service allows you to hide the fact that you are in Central America and it can make it appear you are in the U.S. This is just one example – there are many other video and content-based restrictions of living here.

Secondly, and I am not advocating breaking the law, a VPN service can be used to hide the IP address of those who are downloading and uploading information via bit-torrent sites (peer to peer sharing websites used to share music, movies, software and more), protecting your identity.

CHAPTER 11 – Common questions

Because we write often on our blogs - okay, Jen write
often, I write occasionally – we get a lot of questions
from potential expats and visitors who are planning a
lengthy stay. Here are a couple of the most frequently
asked questions about being an expat here.

93. Can I work here?

It is amazing how many expats forget the negative
feelings they had about immigrants in their home
country working (legally or illegally). Then, when that
expat moves, er, emigrates to Costa Rica…

It is also amazing the number of people who have no
money, but are ready to quit their job and move here,
find work, and start a new life.

It is not that easy.

Costa Rica, like every other country out there, creates
laws protecting work for their citizens. Therefore, it is
difficult for a foreigner to come into the country and
work legally.

There are a few ways to do this, however:

- Become a permanent resident – this takes money,
  and just as important, time. To establish
  permanent residency you must go through two
  rounds of temporary residency (two years equals
  one round). Because it can take over a year to
  receive your first Cedula (greencard) you are

looking at waiting at least five years before you
are able to work.

- Start a business – you may not be able to work
  for someone else, but you can start a business.
  All employees hired must be Tico or legal to
  work in the country and you cannot do the work
  yourself – unless it is a job that a Tico cannot do.

- Get a work visa – if the company you work for
  in the States (or wherever) has an office here and
  they move you to Costa Rica for work, they can
  help you get a work visa so that you can work
  for them, in country, legally.

- Work on-line – this by far is the most popular
  way to earn a living here while skirting the work
  issue. Many write (books, articles, blog posts) or
  have a website that sells a product.

The reality is that working for a company here, most
likely, would not pay the type of money one would
expect as labor, as a whole, is inexpensive here. It is best
for those who wish to move here to be self-sufficient –
either have enough money to live on, have an online
business, or have investments that provide an income.

94. What is the cost of living?

How much will it cost you to live here if you decide to
retire to Costa Rica? Can you live on $1,000, $1,500,
$5,000?

Yes.

The real question is: what kind of lifestyle do you want? Where do you want to live? Are you going to own a car?

If you move to Costa Rica with the mentality that it is simply a cheaper version of the U.S. (or wherever you are from), then not only will you spend the same (or more) than you do now, but you will really miss out on the cultural aspects of living in a foreign country.

The Central Valley is less expensive to live in than the beach areas in just about every category. Not only are the foods and services more expensive in beach areas but rent and home prices will be more expensive as well. Most homes in the Central Valley lack heating and air-conditioning – they just are not needed with the temperate climate of the hills of the Central Valley.

My wife and I live somewhat frugally, we have a beautiful home with a million dollar view, we try to eat healthy – Jen usually achieves this, I do not – and we do not buy too many expensive, imported items, like cheese or prepackaged foods. We go out to eat three or four times a month and take the occasional trip to a beach or a national park. We do not have a car, but rely on public transportation, taxis (rarely), or hire a driver for the day (very rare, only when we have guests).

To give you an idea of a budget for two adults living in the Central Valley, frugally but not too frugally, here is our monthly budget of $1,500 by category:

Rent for a three bed/two bath house
    $625
(includes lawn care and internet)

Groceries (includes household items)
    $500

Transportation
    $100

Utilities (electric/water)
    $75

Dinners Out and Extra
    $200

You will notice that there is not a line item for medications or for health insurance. The health insurance will eventually add a bit to our budget... hopefully, meds never will.

95. Can I drink the water?

One of the great aspects of visiting and living in Costa Rica is that, except for very remote areas of the country, the water is drinkable from the tap.

There is little need to worry about Montezuma's Revenge or having to carry around a water bottle everywhere you go. Fresh, clean water is readily available throughout the country.

Come on in... the water's fine.

96. What do you do all day?

I became Intentionally Unemployed at the age of 41. Coming from a career where I was responsible for all aspects of a company – 40 employees, sales, production, quality, client relations, etc., I had a fear that, when I retired, there would be a void in my life.

Ja ja ja ja (in English – ha ha ha ha).

Like many fears, this one was unfounded. I really think it boils down to this axiom: only boring people get bored. But still, people want to know what a (now) 42-year-old retired person does in Costa Rica to fill his time. Joseph Campbell's quote, "Follow your bliss" sums up the answer to that question quite well.

I now have the time to delve into interests that I did not have time for in the States such as photography, writing, and hiking.

I sound like a dating site profile because I also enjoy long walks in the mountains, watching sunsets with a glass of wine in hand and sunrises with cup of coffee.

The majority of our friends are also retired and have an ample supply of that commodity, time. Because of this we are able to develop deeper friendships and enjoy more social activities than before – so much so that it can be overwhelming.

Jen and I have time to enjoy the sunrise and sunset together and to develop a better relationship with each other.

There are also many volunteer opportunities allowing the expat to give back to his new community. It can be as simple as befriending a Tico and helping them with his English, or helping out at an animal rescue center. There are many helpful ways to use your time.

CHAPTER 12 – Advice and opinions

I saved, for the end, a couple of tips and rants about living here that not all will agree with. The rants are my personal viewpoints and if you disagree that is ok. Basically, they are examples of "Ugly American" behavior that I find embarrassing. These tips and rants are primarily for those who plan to move here, or who at the very least will be staying for a couple of months.

Tourists will typically be in touristy areas, spending tourist dollars and getting treated like tourists. For those living in Costa Rica, you will most likely not be in a touristy area, you will live in close proximity to Tico neighbors, have to deal with government agencies, and eat in restaurants that cater to Costa Ricans not Gringos.

In other words, your experience here will be foreign to you.

Why else would you want to move to another country - just because it is cheaper? I think you will be sorry if that's the case. First off, Costa Rica is not that cheap. In fact it is the most expensive of all the Central American countries. Secondly, if you are not going to celebrate the differences in culture why leave the States at all?

97. Visit first

As my opening sentence of this book shows, a large percentage of people who move to Costa Rica with the intention of living here permanently return home before they reach their first anniversary. The reasons vary, but the main one is lack of knowledge and preparation.

It is easy to read a few blog posts, or a book, and get the impression that Costa Rica is indeed paradise, perfect with no flaws. Maybe you even came here for a week-long vacation, sipped a piña colada on the beach while the sun went down, zip lined through the jungle canopy, fed a baby spider monkey milk out of a bottle, or watched as turtle hatchlings struggled to meet the waves of the ocean in the dead of night.

What better place to live than this, right?

Living here is a whole other story. Instead of doing touristy stuff, your day is filled with waiting for the cable guy to show because he had already blown an appointment (OK, not much different than the U.S.) or calling your attorney for the fourth time in as many days because he will not return your calls. You have bills to pay, things to take care of, groceries to buy, a vehicle to maintain, a budget to keep.

You need to learn if you can live here. Recently on one of the Costa Rica Expat groups on Facebook someone posed a question that went something like this:

"I have heard good things and bad things about Costa Rica. Please shoot straight and tell me which is true."

Well, it's all of the above and so much more. It may be a small country (yes, please remember it's a country) but it is very varied. There are so many different weather patterns (micro-climates) here that you can be literally down the road from a friend and you both experience different weather.

Some areas experience higher crime than others, or you may be in a safe, small farming community, and still get burgled.

The only way to find out if Costa Rica is a fit for you is to do as much research as you can and then come visit. The longer you can stay, the better. Visit different towns and different elevations within those towns. Do it all as if you were living here. Don't go off and do touristy stuff. Instead hunker down, get to know the culture, the neighborhood, and the people.

Don't visit with the expectation that you are in a mini-USA. You will be in a country that has been developing its very own culture for over 800 years. While the technology and many other things you will experience here will remind you of North America, it is not. It is best to leave your preconceptions at home, but pack some patience, a sense of adventure and, most importantly, a sense of humor.

Spend at least a month in each place you are considering to determine if it could be a fit. You may find that you don't really care for living in Costa Rica at all. Good job, your effort has paid off and you just saved a whole lot of money on moving expenses.

98. Rent before buying

There is an often-trumpeted piece of advice given to those moving to Costa Rica: Rent before you buy. It is easy to buy real estate here, even as a visitor, but it can be difficult to sell.

This truth goes a bit deeper. It is true that it is easy to buy property here. And while the transaction requires an attorney, and a realtor is helpful, it is (usually) not a complicated transaction.

It is also true that it can be difficult to sell. There is a glut of expats who fall in lust with a property and buy it only to find out they don't really like Costa Rica, or something about the property, or its neighbors.

This is the real advantage of renting, even if you just can't wait to own property here. By renting in the area in which you want to live – ideally the house you are interested in buying – you get to see what it is really like to live in that neighborhood, its micro-climate, its neighbors, its quirks.

You may just find out that the neighbor next door has, not one, but three hound dogs; a rooster who doesn't start crowing at dawn, but rather, at about 2 a.m.; and that they love to start their day at 6 a.m. with off-tune karaoke to 80's power ballads.

If you haven't guessed, these were one of our first neighbors, and while the house was great and fell within our budget, the neighbors left something to be desired.

Then there is the financial aspect of tying up cash in a home. Borrowing money in Costa Rica is not an option that is available to most expats. Even if it were the interest rate for the loan would not be palatable. A few homes are sold with the seller carrying the note at a reasonable rate, but the reality is most homes are sold for cash.

So, with the favorable interest rates available for those investing money, you could invest the cash you would have tied up in a home and instead rent a home with the proceeds. Say you were going to buy a $150,000 home but instead put it into a six-month CD earning 6% – that is $9,000 a year in interest or a rent payment of $750 a month – which can get you a decent home, at least in the Central Valley, and you won't have to worry about repairs or home upkeep. Then again, you won't own a home of your own either.

The good news for us renters is that there are many houses available where the owners bought, left the country, and can't unload the home. This creates an opportunity to get a great deal on a rental, many times fully furnished.

I am not against home ownership here. It is not right for Jen and me, but it can be for others. It just makes sense to know what you are getting into.

99. Get a great deal on a rental

In general, I put real estate agents on the same pedestal as attorneys – a very low one. This is even truer in Costa

Rica, where transactions involving property are not very well regulated and you have to be very careful with whom you entrust this responsibility.

Another reason to rent before buying. You can get to know the realtor talent in your area and their reputation before you use their services. I now know two in our area that I would trust with any real estate transaction, but it took over a year to determine that.

But unless you know the system, you will need an agent to help buy a piece of property. If you are renting, though, finding a rental on your own through your network will save you money – sometimes big money.

We moved to the Central Valley with just nine suitcases. We had secured an apartment to stay in for our first three months. The apartment was tiny, maybe 400 square feet, with a tiny bed, tiny stove and a tiny refrigerator. But that didn't matter.

In fact, it was probably good that the apartment was less than ideal, as it pushed us to make friends, meet people, and get the word out that we were looking for a rental.

In no time we were put in touch with the owner of a two-bedroom, two-bath home who was just starting to look for renters and realtors did not know about it. The price was $600 a month and was a fit for us. If this were rented through an agent the price would have been closer to $700 as the agent typically charges the first month's rent as their fee.

Also, it is in the agent's best interest to charge as much as they possibly can. New expats to an area have no idea of the real market conditions and if they are basing their idea of a "good deal" on experiences from the States, they will over pay.

In my experience securing a rental yourself will save you money. One last tip regarding rentals: it is common practice for some home owners to keep the renters security deposit at the end of a lease, regardless of the condition the home was left in – you know, as a bonus for the landlord. One method used to combat this unscrupulous practice is to withhold the last month's rent and tell the owner to apply the security deposit. This will be met with anger but at least you don't lose the security deposit (typically one month's rent).

100. Don't be an askhole

There is a popular meme going around that defines the word askhole as "Someone who asks for your advice and then does the exact opposite."

I define it for the potential expat a little differently: "A person who asks uninformed questions, who is needy and ungrateful and takes but doesn't give."

In the world of becoming an expat or a long-term visitor to Costa Rica, you will need to build a network. You will need to ask questions and you will need help and there will be plenty of people to help you. Don't be an askhole. Ask informed questions, don't bug people with questions whose answers are easily found, and when you meet them in person, buy them a beer or lunch and say thanks.

Networking is an important aspect of moving to and living in Costa Rica. If you are an askhole you may find yourself un-networked.

101. Don't be a cheapskate

There is a difference between being frugal and being cheap. And there seems to be a decent number of expats here who are cheap.

It really tweaks my beak when I see expats nickel and diming Ticos – just because they can. I have seen people get upset because they were charged .20 more for their kilo of tomatoes at the farmers market than someone else was. Or complain that they have to pay a Christmas bonus (mandated by law) to their maid who makes $4 an hour.

If this sounds like you, just stay where you are. I don't think Costa Rica is right for you.

102. Don't be THAT guy/girl

See what a nice guy I am? I gave you two extra rants – instead of stopping at 100 I just kept going.

I recently had lunch at a nice restaurant with a friend. As we were chatting and eating, I noticed a couple in the corner of the outdoor seating area and the woman was fidgeting, moving things around the table and looking wildly around the restaurant. You could tell she was in distress.

I was about to walk over to see if she needed help with something when she picked up her empty wine glass, lifted it over her head, and waved it back and forth. I guess she needed a refill.

This display of what some call the Ugly American is played out every day here. I know this is how some act in the U.S. when they perceive that they are not getting adequate service – typically in restaurants. These people, rightfully so, many times get added condiments on their food, free of charge.

The sad part is two-fold. First, I knew the lady and was embarrassed for her and because of her. Secondly, it brought back memories of a few times where I acted that way in the States and, once again, was embarrassed to be That Guy.

I will tell you up front that, unless you are in a tourist area, your experience of customer service here will be much different than the service you get in the States. Once again, knowing what to expect will help you cope with the differences.

Whether you are an expat living in Costa Rica, or a visitor on vacation, remember this is not your country, this is not your culture so, relax.

Okay, I will get off my soapbox now and wrap this book up.

FINAL THOUGHTS

There is an acronym in use on the Internet today, and it could very well be Costa Rica's national motto:

YMMV – Your Mileage May Vary.

Taken from the auto-industry, the saying basically means that everyone's experiences will be different.

This was one of the most frustrating things in researching living in Costa Rica. We would read an account on a forum of how to accomplish something and the thread would blow up and name-calling would commence because someone (or many others) had a different experience of the same scenario. The hilarious part is that everyone was right – they all experienced different outcomes of the same scenario.

Whether it was a border crossing for a 90-day visa stamp, being stopped at customs when flying into the country, opening a bank account, or one of any number of things, whatever you read may not resemble the experience you actually might have.

The most important things we brought with us to Costa Rica were: a sense of adventure, a boatload of patience, and a willingness to laugh and find humor in the things that did not go as we had planned.

My hope with this book is to provide you with our experiences and observations of many different aspects of life here. But don't make the mistake of thinking that the way I describe a situation is the only way you might experience it.

Your Mileage Will Vary.

Bonus Round

I am a big fan of free, so I have included two freebies on the following pages.

But first, a word from our sponsor:

I hope you found value in, and enjoyed, this book. Please consider writing a review on Amazon. Reviews are critical to the success of a book.

If you have any questions about living in or visiting Costa Rica shoot me an email. I still have the remnants of response time from my working days and people are typically amazed that: one, I reply and two, I reply quickly.

I don't always know the answer, but if not I can usually point you to resources.

CostaRicaCurious@icloud.com

BONUS 1 – 50 Tiquismos
Costa Rica Specific Slang

A cachet – Same as Pura Vida.

Bicho: A bug or creepy crawly. Be careful: in some Latin American countries Bicho refers to a part of a male's anatomy.

Birra: Beer.

Birrear: To drink beer.

Boca: An appetizer, sometimes given as a freebee to start your meal, or as a free snack at a bar.

Bodega: Warehouse or storage area.

Buena Nota: Person of note; a cool person.

Chunche: A thingee or object.

Cigarette chinga: Cigarette butt.

Comedera: Food or groceries.

¿Cómo amaneció?: How are you doing this morning?

Di/diay: Used at the beginning of a sentence as filler, similar to "um" or "well."

Dolor de jupa: Headache.

Estar de goma: To suffer from a hangover.

Fut: Short for futbol (soccer for you USA'ians).

Guila: A child.

Ingrato: An ungrateful person.

Jamar: To eat.

Jumas: To be drunk.

La choza: Home.

La vara: The thing.

Mae or Maj: Used the same way N. Americans use "dude" or "man."

Mala Nota: Very bad. Not cool.

Mucho gusto: Translates directly as "(with) much pleasure." Costa Ricans use this in lieu of "de nada" in response to thank you.

No entender ni papa: To not understand a word.

Ojo: Watch out.

Pachanga: Party.

Por dicha: Thank goodness.

Pulpe or pulpería: A small corner store.

Pura vara: Lies.

Pura vida: The Costa Ricans laidback philosophy of life. Can mean anything from "take it easy" to "it is what it is."

Qué chiva: How cool.

Qué cuentos: Yeah, right.

Qué mala nota: What a bad person.

Qué pereza: Ugh, what a drag.

Qué torta: What a mess.

¿Qué micha?: What's up? What do you have to tell me?

Un rojo: A 1000 colón bill.

Salado/a: Unlucky or "too bad."

Saludos: Greetings.

Soda: A small, typically family-run restaurant.

Solo Bueno: Directly translated as "Only Good," but frequently used to indicate "All is well" or as a description for a product describing it as the "best."

Soque: Hurry up (when speaking).

Típico: Native in style i.e., Comida Típica (traditional food)

Tuanis: Used the same way N. Americans use "cool" – ¡Tuanis Mae!

Tome chichi: A teasing form of "take that."

Una teja: 100 of anything, usually money (100 colones). For directions it means one block (100 meters).

Upe: The Costa Rican doorbell. Most homes do not have a doorbell and have fences and gates so visitors will announce themselves by shouting, "Upe" – over and over again.

Viejo rabo verde: A dirty old man.

BONUS 2 – A chapter from *Costa Rica Chica*

Here is one of the chapters from my wife's book *Costa Rica Chica*. In the book, Jen tells the story of how we came to consider retiring early as well as covering our due diligence trip, prepping to move, and finally, our first three months in Costa Rica.

Costa Rica Chica is available on Amazon as an eBook and in soft-cover.

Here is the free chapter:

3. Dreaming of 50 cent beer

Soon after Greg and I had started officially dating, Richard took me aside one day and said, "Jen, I want you to know, that of all my sons, Greg is the romantic one."

I knew this. But now, after all these years, I really know that Greg is truly romantic – and kind, intuitive and, well, just a huge sweetheart.

As well as being romantic, my husband has always been a dreamer. Being a dreamer means you're optimistic, always thinking of different things and new options – thinking for yourself and not just what someone taught you. Dreamers are usually very artistic and romantic, and Greg is all of these things.

Nobody is perfect, however, and we've had some trials

and tribulations along the way, but I feel like we have something special that few people have. The older I get, the more I respect him. He makes me feel that I am truly the luckiest girl in the world.

Anyway (now that y'all feel warm and fuzzy), it is not unusual for Greg to tell me his dreams. And by dreams, I don't mean the sleeping kind, but fully awake daytime dreams. I also have learned through the course of our marriage not to get too excited about these dreams or jump up and down and say, "Yes, that's a *great* idea – let's do that right away!" – because, trust me, he would take me at my word and be off implementing said dream in a heartbeat!

It's not unusual for Greg to come home from work and start into a conversation right away with, "Jen, I've been thinking… ," which is when I know to brace myself for a who-knows-what kind of dream. One time he was ready to quit his job and leave me for six months to hike the Appalachian Trail. Granted, that sounded pretty cool (I love hiking too), and he *did* ask me to come with him, but someone had to stay home and pay the bills. Luckily that dream faded away, and I wasn't going to bring it up again.

Another time he came home from work and told me all about his plan to quit his job and start a door-to-door mobile dry cleaning service. I was beginning to see a pattern here – all his ideas started with him quitting his job.

Greg and I are good for each other and tend to balance

each other out. Sometimes I do go along with his spontaneity and dreams, and we have a blast. But more times than not we end up talking things through, the pros and the cons, and discover that the dream *might* be a good idea, but first, let's see how things pan out and whether we really want to pursue it or not. In other words, maybe if we wait for a while, the dream will be forgotten.

One night, as we were lying in bed, each reading our own book, I asked Greg what he was reading.

He said, "Well, actually it's an e-book by Tim Leffel called *The World's Cheapest Destinations*. It's quite interesting – about the best and cheapest places to live throughout the world."

This didn't faze me at all, knowing what a dreamer he is, but I proceeded to ask him the dutiful-wife question of *why*, and he told me, "I've been researching and reading different articles lately; and maybe, just maybe, this is my way out. *Our* way out. A way for us to retire early and not have to work... ."

I was perking up now. "Really? How could we possibly quit our jobs and not have to work? Not sure I'm following you."

"I know it sounds odd," he said, "but seriously, I think there is a way we could do it. But here's the thing: we can't do it in the United States. The taxes and healthcare are too outrageously expensive here."

Hmmmmmmm," I replied (which is code for: ARE YOU CRAZY??).

Prior to this point, we had carefully thought through the possibility of Greg quitting his job and taking a job elsewhere or doing something different, but he felt like he would just be trading one stressful management job for another, and he wasn't trained for any other type of industry. He would have to start all over again.

He had thought about starting his own business, but there is always a lot of start-up money needed for that, and also there is always a chance of it failing, as many first-time businesses do. That just seemed too risky at this point in our lives.

Hearing for the first time this "quit our jobs and move to a foreign country" from Greg, I treated it like just another one of his dreams that he is really into at the moment. I felt quite certain it would never come to fruition. I mean, come on! How could we quit our jobs and give up our income at this stage in our lives?

Just for grins, however, and because I didn't want him to think I wasn't taking him seriously, I asked him, "Okay, so where in the world are decent, cheap places to live?"

Greg replied, "It says here that you can get a 50-cent beer in Panama."

"Oh, that's a *great* reason, hon!" (code for: YOU CANNOT BE SERIOUS).

Greg just smiled, ignored my sarcasm, and plugged on,

"Look, it says Panama is friendly to Americans, ever since the U.S. finished building the Panama Canal in 1914. The form of currency is the U.S. dollar, and English is widely spoken, although Spanish is the main language. There is also Ecuador – I was just reading that rent and food are supposed to be very cheap there."

"Hmmmmm," I replied again (this time code for: YOU HONESTLY THINK WE COULD DO THIS?).

He told me to just sleep on it for a while.

So, I fell asleep that night dreaming of all the free time I would have from not spending forty-plus hours a week in my little cubicle.

Greg fell asleep dreaming of cheap beer.

25574153R00092

Made in the USA
Middletown, DE
04 November 2015